REFEATHERING THE EMPTY NEST

REFEATHERING THE EMPTY NEST

Life After the Children Leave

Wendy Aronsson

ROWMAN & LITTLEFIELD
Lanham • Boulder • New York • Toronto • Plymouth, UK

Published by Rowman & Littlefield
4501 Forbes Boulevard, Suite 200, Lanham, Maryland 20706
www.rowman.com

10 Thornbury Road, Plymouth PL6 7PP, United Kingdom

British Library Cataloguing in Publication Information Available

Library of Congress Cataloging-in-Publication Data

Aronsson, Wendy, 1958–
Refeathering the empty nest : life after the children leave / Wendy Aronsson
pages cm
Includes bibliographical references and index.
ISBN 978-1-4422-2402-5 (cloth : alk. paper) — ISBN 978-1-4422-2403-2 (electronic)
1. Parents. 2. Empty nesters. 3. Parenting. I. Title.
HQ755.8.A7324 2014
306.874—dc23
2013051338

∞™ The paper used in this publication meets the minimum requirements of American National Standard for Information Sciences Perma-
nence of Paper for Printed Library Materials, ANSI/NISO Z39.48-1992.

Printed in the United States of America

To my husband Jeffry and two sons
Michael and William,
whose love and support inspired me
to write this book
Our nest is the greatest source of joy in my life
With my eternal love and gratitude

CONTENTS

ACKNOWLEDGMENTS

With love and appreciation to my mother, Peggy, and late father, Billy, whose love and encouragement have been an inspiration to me. To my sister, Nancy, for her insights, contributions, and support. To Aunt Gillian and Uncle Charles, who have cheered me on from the inception of writing this book. To Nancy Steiner, whose unwavering support, wisdom, and tenacity have contributed enormously to this book. For her loyalty and friendship, I will be forever grateful. To Meredith Vieira for taking the time to make herself available to me and for her candor, humor, and thoughtful input. To Janai Lowenstein for her generous contributions. To Debbi O'Shea for her humor, candor, and encouragement from the inception.

For all those who generously contributed their stories and time: Thank you for your honesty, humor, and support, important elements to the substance of this book.

To my agent, Maryann Karinch, of The Rudy Agency, thank you for your wisdom, support, and invaluable contributions.

Thank you to the publishing team at Rowman & Littlefield, and particularly editor Suzanne Staszak-Silva.

DISCLAIMER

The cases described in this book are based on real incidents. However, except as specified, names and specific details have been changed at the request of interviewees who wish to remain anonymous. Therefore, any likeness that might be found with any living individual, except as specified, is unintended.

INTRODUCTION: PURPOSE OF THE BOOK AND SOURCES OF INSIGHTS

Starting with the baby boomers (born between 1946 and 1964), several generations of parents are facing challenges that distinguish us from parents representing previous generations. For parents born after World War II, a life phase I call "the Shift" has taken shape and is an outgrowth of a step change in the style of parenting that many people have embraced—a style reflecting increased involvement in our children's lives as well as a great deal of deliberateness in how we've raised our children. Because of this increased involvement, the challenge presented by the Shift is adjusting to the extent to which the departure of our children from the nest affects us. The associated opportunity is how we have laid the foundation for continued connection with our children and the cultivation of possibilities for our own future.

I wrote this book because the Shift necessitates looking at the nest from a 360-degree perspective. Looking all around, going full circle in seeing what's around you, means that you can start to see all of the fibers interwoven in your nest—and to realize that it is evolving rather than empty. They are the fibers of your relationships, curiosity, accomplishments, feelings, plans, and much more. Hopefully, this book will help you position yourself to gain that 360-degree perspective—to help you explore and understand your feelings and reflections, and to gain resolution from insights about this phase of life.

Much like the information in books such as *Passages* and *What to Expect When You're Expecting,* this book addresses shared life experiences. It suggests what the commonalities might be about this particular life phase.

There are, however, some key differences, including other areas of life I've explored with this book. A theme running throughout the book is the importance of sifting through the research and stories to determine what is or is not useful in others' experiences and information. In this book, you may closely identify with some stories because you have lived through what the person is describing; the feelings and responses expressed by the individual resonate for you. In contrast, you may also have moments when you don't relate to the experiences described. Depending on personal circumstances, family situations, and relationships with children, there are tremendous variances in how we feel and behave as we help our young adults leave home and the impact it has on us, and then become accustomed to life without day-to-day parenting. This phase of life embodies a paradox: Countless numbers of us are experiencing the same events, yet we don't experience them the same way. Hundreds of people contributed their insights and stories to this book, which also weaves in research about the evolution of family life in the late twentieth and early twenty-first centuries. In addition to interviews with many individuals, I also conducted web-based surveys to find out what a broad spectrum of people had to say about their emotions and behavior related to the time of life leading up to and encompassing the departure of young adults from the home.

The answers and comments that survey respondents volunteered about their style of parenting, initial feelings when their young adults left, communication habits with their young adults, and so much more gave a good sense of some of both the commonalities and differences in what parents in this phase of life are experiencing.

Although in the same age group, the respondents did not fall into the same categories in terms of education, income, or location:

- Ninety-five percent were between the ages of forty-five and sixty, with a handful in their early sixties.
- They reported household income as follows:

$0–$24,999	15%
$25,000–$49,999	12%
$50,000–$99,999	26%
$100,000–$149,999	25%
$150,000+	22%

- In terms of education, 90 percent of the respondents had at least a college degree:

Less than high school degree	1%
High school degree	9%
Some college	27%
Associate or bachelor degree	34%
Graduate degree	29%

- The geographic distribution of respondents went from coast to coast:

New England	5%
Middle Atlantic	14%
East North Central	15%
West North Central	3%
South Atlantic	17%
East South Central	10%
West South Central	6%
Mountain	10%

Pacific   20%

Respondents to the web-based surveys had the opportunity to provide narrative remarks in addition to selecting answers to multiple-choice questions, and many generously provided additional insights about their circumstances. Some were single parents noting the significant involvement of a grandparent or unmarried partner in raising their children. Some talked about financial challenges that put a strain on the family and affected their parenting. It is differences such as these that enrich the number of variables related to the "evolving nest" phase of life and make it so potentially unpredictable in terms of feelings and behaviors.

The real stories captured in this book often do more than describe responses to the different stages of the life phase I call the Shift. Many also point the way to possibilities for the future. Hopefully, some of these stories will not only provide comfort and insights, but also plant seeds in your imagination and help you envision the kind of life you want after your young adults leave the nest.

The book is a three-part progression: first, expressing characteristics of the Shift; next, looking at the array of emotions and circumstances that can be realities of the Shift; and finally, addressing the journey toward life after the Shift. This last section is about both possibilities and unexpected changes in the way the nest evolves. The possibilities are endless. The unexpected changes tend to fall into only two categories: the young adult makes a round-trip and comes back home and/or older parents or relatives need regular attention and perhaps financial support.

Regardless of how your Shift progresses, there are insights to be found here in true stories and research that will hopefully help you understand some aspect of what you are experiencing and where you are headed on your journey. All of the contributors to this book gave generously of their time and information to support you through the Shift. Similarly, my purpose in writing this book is to provide information, support, and understanding about an important phase of life's journey.

I

About the Shift

I

PARENTING IN THE EVOLVING NEST

> How many hopes and fears, how many ardent wishes and anxious apprehensions are twisted together in the threads that connect the parent with the child!
> —Samuel G. Goodrich, *Recollections of a Lifetime*, 1857

The wall calendar read "June." I flipped the page; there was no "July."

This was my younger son's high school calendar, with the dates of games, parent-teacher meetings, and school holidays. I took it down and thought about keeping it, since there would never be another high school calendar in this house again.

And then I realized, "This is the Shift." The end of school calendars signifies the end of a time when I will know what's happening day to day in my children's lives. It's a subtle reminder of a big change. Whatever calendars I might have from now on will look a whole lot different. After a little reflection, I threw away the high school calendar.

When my older son graduated from high school, the changes in our nest were not as dramatic. We still had schedules that included academic, social, and extracurricular activities—and a calendar that highlighted many of them. Yet in subtle ways, his departure awakened me to an imminent journey, prompting me to write this book to illuminate the challenges and opportunities associated with "the Shift," a time of continuous evolution in the lives of parents and their young adults.

Just as our younger son was taking great strides toward independence as a college freshman, our older son moved into the next stage of his life. He finished college, secured employment, and moved into his first post-college apartment, which he chose himself and furnished on his own. He was launched and on his way to adulthood.

While there was a great deal of excitement and fulfillment in watching those developments in our older son's life, it was the younger son's departure that signaled the fact that my husband and I were experiencing the Shift.

Being a parent has been among the most gratifying, challenging, and growth-inducing aspects of my life. I have hoped that this next life phase would involve discovery, fulfillment, and contribution in other areas of my life; the research and writing of this book were among those areas. As a psychotherapist, I am aware that some parents quickly move toward new opportunities for growth after their young adults leave home, while others struggle to see what possibilities lay beyond day-to-day parenting. Hopefully, the stories, studies, and insights in the book will shed light on the variances in the change process from one person to another.

Even after decades of experience as a therapist—reading volumes, listening to thousands of stories, exchanging ideas with colleagues—I still could not predict how my own responses to launching my children would take shape. It did not preclude me from taking my own journey, with many of the challenges others had described to me as their nests evolved. Facing my own circuitous path made me even more attuned to what other people were experiencing as they went through the Shift. Millions of parents are concurrently moving through the same phase of life, with feelings, perceptions, and behavior that might be quite similar in some ways, but in others, quite different.

Roughly twenty-five million people in the United States are classified as "empty nesters," that is, people who have no children living in their home post-graduation from high school.[1] Only a little more than half of those—and this is based on both surveys and studies—say that they consider themselves emotionally prepared for no longer having children at home.[2] This is not surprising considering that they are experiencing a new life passage. In one study, 23 percent indicated profound unhappiness when their young adults left.[3] In contrast to that, several studies have suggested that the transition to an empty nest is much easier than previous research had suggested and that "many parents get a new lease on life when their children leave."[4]

In short, the evidence seems to be conflicting, and there may be good reasons why this is so. In understanding the data, it's important to acknowledge that feelings about having the youngest child move out may differ markedly from one parent to another, and those feelings may vacillate daily.

SIGNS THE NEST IS EVOLVING

Parenthood begins when you decide to have a child. Sometimes the first step is easy: You (or your partner) get pregnant. Often it's filled with stress and paperwork because you rely on in vitro fertilization, surrogacy, or adoption. Regardless of the method you use to become a parent, your focus early on is welcoming a child into your home. You choose to change your life.

Actually, you choose to change your life repeatedly. But one of the changes you probably don't think about in those early days of welcoming and raising your children is the change and challenge as they transition to adulthood. The challenge is having to establish a new equilibrium after a shift from the status quo.

The first change occurs in the months of waiting for the child, when you have time to read everything you can get your hands on about preparing to have a child and then what to do immediately after the child arrives. This preparation sets the stage for continued, informed parenting and it separates us from prior generations of parents. As of 2013, prospective mothers and fathers had more than 32,000 books on pregnancy to choose from and more than 100,000 books on the topic of child development.[5] Curious about how many books the parents of baby boomers had on the subjects, I asked the senior librarian at an area library, who said she would research the topic and call later with an answer. When Maggie did call back, she laughed and said, "A few Gerber Baby [Foods] books and Dr. Spock." She assured me this was not a glib response, but rather a summary statement after digging through archives to try to unearth a specific answer.

Her research validates one of the key differences in parenting since the World War II generation of parents. The number of resources offering expert advice about pregnancy and child-rearing has shown exponential growth in the generations since World War II. That growth reflects the dramatic rise in breakthrough studies and published works on the human psyche and human biology. For example, in the early part of the twentieth century, Sigmund Freud, Carl Jung, and B. F. Skinner held dominant roles in discussions of human behavior; however, between the mid-1960s and end of the century, hundreds of important new thought leaders and studies emerged. Many of them focused on child development, such as Anna Freud's study of the psychology of children[6]; the work of many researchers, most notably Mary Ainsworth, in the area of children's attachment styles[7]; and Simon Baron-Cohen's theories on autism.[8]

With the arrival of a child, a tidal wave of changes occurs in rapid succession. The interaction of the couple transforms when they go from a dyad to a triad, from focusing on each other to putting much, or even most, of their attention on a child. In the case of a single parent, she suddenly has to be "other focused," so the experience of downtime or personal time may be almost non-existent. The spectrum of emotions and dynamic nature of raising a child means that life in the nest is never static. With the imminent departure of a child, the changes of the Shift can be quite subtle—like the calendar—in contrast to bringing a squealing infant into your home. The Shift affects both women and men, although they may experience it differently. The notion that men can automatically go through the Shift unaffected emotionally is not accurate. Unlike their fathers, men belonging to the Baby Boomer generation ushered in a new level of involvement in their children's lives. They took classes in helping their partners with labor, donned a hospital gown and actively took part in the birth, as opposed to sitting in a room, waiting for a nurse to fling open a door and announce: "It's a boy!" For many, that level of interest in their child's life and well-being never abated.

My friend's husband came home last Sunday after a business trip and expected to play golf with his son—something they did every Sunday. The son had decided he wanted to stay in the city with some friends Saturday night, so when he came home, he was too tired to play golf. The dad went to play alone, which he did periodically anyway. A friend at the golf course asked, "Where's your son?"

"He blew me off."

"Get used to that."

When my friend's husband told her that story, her eyes lit up as we had been talking about the Shift. Now she had a name to put to the myriad life changes she was starting to see. She told him, "Aha! You're feeling the Shift, too."

He dismissed her conclusion and said, "I did not say anything about getting used to an interruption in our standing golf game." But the reality is this: The very fact that the remark resonated with him enough to come home and tell his wife is an indication that he's experiencing the Shift. He may be feeling it subtly, but he is feeling it.

The golf game and the calendar signal an irreversible change in the status quo. What once was a usual practice is now part of the past. Some of the routines might occur so far below your radar that it will take months or years for you to realize they no longer occur. Maybe you and your daughter used to chat in detail about what she planned to do in the coming week—an informal, but regular, routine. That stopped when she went to college. You still talk, but the details about friends and school are gone.

As busy as he is, even President Barack Obama has a sense that, as his children go through their teenage years, he and the first lady are facing changes in their relationship with Malia and Sasha. In an August 23, 2013, interview, President Obama talked about his realization that his daughters were becoming more independent: "What I'm discovering is that each year, I get more excited about spending time with them, they get a little less excited. . . . I think there is an element from Michelle and me, we see what's coming." Even though they were only twelve and fifteen years old at the time of the interview, their school activities, sports practices, and other interests were keeping them occupied outside the home more and more. The president and first lady had an increasing awareness that their days of daily parenting would come to an end someday.[9]

By reading this book, you will hopefully take a step back to gain perspective on your day-to-day life and recognize some of those moments and routines that are changing. It is part of becoming aware of how the nest is evolving and what kind of challenges and rewards come along with that progression. The tinge of emptiness that may accompany this awareness can work both ways, of course, and there will likely be some attempt by both the parent and child to reestablish the status quo. For right now, though, let's keep the focus on what you as a parent are experiencing.

When the routines get interrupted, the natural tendency is to try to restore them. When your eighteen-year-old asks, "Hey, Mom, when you're out, could you please pick up some toothpaste and deodorant for me?" he isn't necessarily trying to test the waters to see how much you'll do for him. On some level, he may be attempting to maintain the status quo. He has a driver's license now, but up to the time when he was able to drive and have some independence, Mom always got the bathroom supplies and various other items; it was a normal part of life at home.

After your young adult has moved out and comes back for visits, it's natural to want to make meals and have conversations just like they used to be. And from the young adult's perspective, it's just as natural to dump his laundry near the washer when he comes home and ask you to pick up some Fritos. Homecomings often are a time when you make de facto moves to return to status quo; they can be a conscious and/or an unconscious effort to re-create patterns. It's not a regression, but rather a common reaction to return to a natural rhythm of what was.

Even though being back in the previous familial configuration lends itself to returning to the way things were, forcing all the new elements of your family life into the same old box can be challenging. These young adults have been making their own choices about drinking and staying out late, and parents are forced to recalibrate what is acceptable in their nest. You aim to identify and maintain familiar parameters that felt comfortable for your nest, yet you also seek to recognize your acceptance of their emerging adulthood. It's a Goldilocks challenge: You are not quite sure what it should be, only that you don't want to end up with something too hard or too soft.

The Shift continues in ebbs and flows. Because of that, you are like a bridge that can only sustain high winds if flexible enough to move with them, yet must remain firm and strong enough to provide stability.

WHAT IS "THE SHIFT?"

As the first generation for which parenting was more of a choice than an expectation, we brought a set of life skills and experiences to parenting that are quite different from that of previous generations. Many of us started families while being involved in a career, so it was only natural that we brought a perspective and experience that lends itself to informed parenting. More so than prior generations, we delved into parenting with the intent to learn as much as possible. There are books and support groups on how to be the best parent you can be, as well as endless resources for parents with specific needs, such as sibling issues, learning differences, or children with food allergies.

We have developed what I call *Precision Parenting*—purposeful, mindful, and deliberate parenting—and as a result, the Shift can be a potentially jarring transition. The Shift is a phenomenon of our twenty-first century society that is new and enduring. It's a pervasive phenomenon that was unidentified and only marginally experienced by previous generations.

When mentioning the subject of my book to a family friend who gave birth to her two daughters during the 1950s, she asked, "What's the big deal?" She didn't go through the Shift and does not see this life phase as representing a uniquely challenging time in the life of a parent. In bygone days when my friend was raising her family, parenthood often began in a person's twenties, which was the case with her, and parenting advice came from the previous generations. Just past middle-age, with perhaps decades of life still ahead of them, parents became grandparents. The nest was always filled with children.

With the baby boomers came choices about the timing of parenthood. Delays in starting a family mean that this generation is faced with the real prospect of having years alone after the children move out. Or they are parents who now find themselves without their children at home, but are confronted with the challenges of taking care of the older generation. An increasing number find themselves with the dual challenge of caring for parents *and* having their young adults move back home until they can generate financial independence. This subject is explored in depth in chapter 8, "Return to the Nest."

With the baby boomers also came myriad opportunities to learn about parenting. Parents, grandparents, and Dr. Spock didn't disappear, but as I referenced above, they had plenty of company from author/experts and family counselors. From T. Berry Brazelton's *Touchpoints* to Haim Ginott's *Between Parent and Child*, the shelves began to fill with parenting advice. Support groups sprang up. More and more therapists began to specialize in working with families.

Precision Parenting as evolved by the baby boomers involves more than curiosity about how to parent skillfully; it's more like parenting artfully, and to some extent, it reflects the fact that many of us had professional lives before we ventured into parenthood. We pursued parenting with the same vigor we brought to our major in college or the first job on our career path. We had already felt internal and cultural pressure to perform well, so it was only natural that we would want to parent well, too. Motivation to excel in raising our children brings about substantial emotional and financial investment. But keep in mind that "substantial" is a relative term. Precision Parenting is diverse and pervasive; it occurs at every socioeconomic level and in a variety of communities.

A study completed in 2012 by researchers at the University of Virginia's Institute for Advanced Studies in Culture looked at different ways to define American parents and came up with four categories: The Faithful Parent, Engaged Progressives, The Detached, and The American Dreamer. The largest group is American Dreamers. Their description of this category captures the essence of what I see as benefits of Precision Parenting. The parents in the American Dreamers category "tend to be optimistic about their children's opportunities and schooling. Insofar as their children are concerned, they hope for much and invest even more, pouring themselves fully into their families' futures."[10] Despite the trying economic times during the period when the study was conducted, parents who can be described as American Dreamers even feel that their children will achieve financial success, according to a separate study conducted by Charles Schwab. About 85 percent of those interviewed expect their young adults to be at least as financially successful as they are.[11] In other words, their optimism for their children's future far exceeds the projections of financial analysts. The latter are looking strictly at economic conditions and trends, whereas the American Dreamers are focused on reasons to be hopeful about their children's future. A primary reason is that they have invested heavily in their children's future success (and this is the thread running throughout Precision Parenting) and so these parents remain hopeful that their investment will yield results.

It is important to understand that there is a distinction between "helicopter parent," a term first used in a 1990 book by Foster Cline and Jim Fay[12] and popularized in the early twenty-first century, and my concept of Precision Parenting. Some parents might show characteristics of both, and the terms are not interchangeable.

A 2012 study in the *Journal of Marriage and Family* describes the style of parenting associated with so-called helicopter parents as "intense parental support."[13] The researchers from Purdue, Pennsylvania State, University of Michigan, University of Texas-Austin, and the University of Pennsylvania studied parental behaviors in order to arrive at their determination of what constitutes "intense parental support." They concluded that nearly 30 percent of parents reported providing intense support for at least one of their grown children—and it was considered "intense" because they provided advice as well as financial, emotional, social, and other types of support many times a week. Twenty-one percent of young adults reported receiving this type of support.

The major difference between the helicopter parent and the precision parent lies in the phrase "intense support." I characterize the type of support provided by precision parents as purposeful and mindful, rather than intense. By definition, "intense" means "extreme." In contrast, "purposeful" means "focused," and in this case, focused on an outcome: the well-being of the child.

The distinction is grounded in problem-solving. A helicopter parent will "land" in the child's life whenever a solution is needed. A precision parent would be more inclined to use a method that is more focused on discovery. One such method is the Socratic approach; that is, to have a conversation with the child that points the way toward a solution, or perhaps to do research related to the issue at hand. It is more a matter of bringing information and organization to a trying situation rather than stepping in and fixing it for the child. It would not be fair to say that either the Socratic or research approach are the only possible ways to engender problem-solving, however.

Because of their laser-like concentration on parenting with excellence, precision parents may feel significantly impacted when the young adult moves out because a focal point of their daily lives is gone. What if you had a career that was part of your identity, part of your spirit, and then you realized you'd have to retire in a few years—or that your job description had been so substantially rewritten that you weren't sure what to do? The Shift starts when that awareness of having to readjust your thinking about parenthood starts to affect you—how you relate to your child, your parenting partner, and your own parents.

By nature, Precision Parenting illustrates a difference from parenting of previous generations. Birth control enabled us to become "deliberate parents" rather than consider parenting a normative experience. Other science, research, technology, and so on gave us the ability to have biological children through new means, including in vitro fertilization, surrogacy, and sperm/egg donation. All of those processes, as well as adoption, involve such an enormous amount of planning and preparation that the prospective parents' schedule revolves around the child long before the child is conceived.

That predisposition to use all of the resources available to us to be informed parents—our time, energy, focus, and dedication to parenthood—can set us up for strong, conflicting feelings when our children are poised to leave the home. Whether it hits us suddenly or we have a creeping awareness of it, when we go from parenting a child to parenting a young adult, we can face some enormous challenges. Of the 100-plus parents who contributed insights and/or stories to this book, many offered versions of the following sentiment, expressed by a woman who gave up her legal career to be with her children full-time: "I felt that at least part of my identity was tied in the role of being a mother, as though that, as the role transformed, I would feel less like a mother. I wondered how I would fill the void and if I would feel worthwhile." But even though the Shift might seem like a time of gaps—gaps in our schedule, gaps in our relationships, and much more—it's also an opportunity to see those gaps as portals to a new life.

The Shift is not just a minor phase you're working through. It is a major life change, even though it is not an abrupt change. It happens gradually, taking shape as series of events on a continuum.

THE NEW NEST

People react differently to the concept of the empty nest. Someone listening in to a group of mothers having lunch together may hear a spectrum of reactions to the very thought of the departure of their children. Here's a sampling:

- "I'm so excited—I'll be able to travel with my husband."
- "This seems so unnatural. I've built my life around my children."
- "We enjoy having them at home. Wish we could have them forever."
- "My nest isn't empty! I am so much more than my children. I'm annoyed when people refer to it."

As that last statement suggests, "empty nest" has a negative connotation. It implies a sense of loss. Instead, I characterize it as the "evolving nest." At the beginning of this chapter, I identified signs that the nest is evolving. In the next chapter, it becomes clear how different people experience that ongoing change in the home environment and familial relationships.

In some cases, the experiences are quite disconcerting. During the Shift, many people have described a struggle with identifying and understanding their changing feelings. Sometimes, they even feel out of touch with their own behavior. To help them conceptualize what they are experiencing, I often use three animals as points of reference: hummingbird, stunned deer, and eager beaver.

Hummingbirds whirl around, flapping their wings dozens of times every second. They fly backward as efficiently as they fly forward, pursuing sources of nectar all around them.[14] The human behaving like a hummingbird keeps busy constantly, moving from project to project and place to place. That kind of frenetic behavior can often be a way of distracting oneself from sadness or anxiety. Temporarily, the heightened level of activity may take the person's mind off of a sense of loss.

In contrast, a stunned deer can't move. I read a story a few years ago that describes the condition in the extreme. A stunned deer stood motionless on a highway for half an hour, staring at the oncoming headlights, until a police officer stopped traffic and carried the young doe to the side of the road.[15] Some experiences in the Shift elicit an analogous response from parents, who become frightened and nearly paralyzed by the changes in their lives, unable to move ahead with the times and the changes. They aren't exactly like the stunned deer, standing on the road in a frozen state and waiting to be rescued, but they do experience some paralyzing emotions, such as disbelief, fear, and uncertainty, that cause them to stop in their tracks, finding it hard to move forward.

The eager beaver is industrious and constructive—a great builder. A person who voraciously reads books with self-help information and insights into the parenting and other life changes in the Shift can be seen as the eager beaver. She wants to learn everything there is to know about building a new nest, redesigning the nest, or launching her young.

It's important to keep in mind that you can be each one at different times. Your responses to the changes in your life as a parent will likely morph, perhaps even from day to day. You may identify clearly as one animal today, but that may be very different from how you see yourself tomorrow. As part of the metamorphosis in your life, it's common to have a sense of being disoriented. Part of that stems from no longer having the same kind of control you used to have over your nest and events in your children's lives.

The Shift is not predictable, and neither are your responses to it. This is not a formulaic life event that can be planned moment-by-moment like a commencement. There will be surprises and inscrutable moments that engender discovery.

THOUGHTS TO CONSIDER

Roughly twenty-five million people in the United States have children who are no longer living at home following graduation from high school. Their experiences are as varied as the number of families. At the same time, all of these parents have this important life event in common.

The parenting styles that emerged after World War II gave rise to an array of new experiences related to launching young adults. This phenomenon has turned what was a milestone of parenting into a life phase—the Shift. Though diverse, parents experiencing the Shift can offer each other valuable insights about this life phase. In this chapter, I began to suggest what those insights might be.

A constructive way to move through the Shift is to shift with it. This requires conscious recognition of the Shift and awareness of the need to alter familiar patterns of thinking established over the long period of time that began with the birth of your first child. One way to start is by looking at the changes that may be occurring now in your life, or are about to occur. Becoming more aware of the types of changes happening in your nest may immediately shed light on what your next steps will be in your journey.

For example, signs the nest is beginning to evolve include tangible evidence: The high school calendar is gone and printouts of college applications are on the kitchen table. Give some thought to the kind of tangible evidence that might remind you of the opportunities you have now that your children have departed. Perhaps you can start to read a book about a subject that has always fascinated you. Or maybe you invest in a new tennis racket to replace the one that's been collecting cobwebs in your closet.

Events in your nest are also taking on a new shape. Routines are disrupted, with young adults sometimes not present during family meals. They are out with their friends more frequently and making independent decisions about how to spend their free time. The counterpart to that is that since they require less of your time, you can now add new events to your life. An invitation to a charity luncheon in the city arrives and, for the first time in years, you are able to attend. You sign up for a weekly yoga class, or decide to take cooking lessons.

New people are coming into your young adult's life as well as your own. The young adult exchanges texts with the person who will be a roommate at the dorm or others who will be attending the same school. At the same time, you may start communicating with other parents who have a young adult planning to go to the same college as your son or daughter. After the launch, your chances to reinvigorate existing relationships can also flourish. You spontaneously arrange for a weekend away with your spouse or partner. You call a friend and make plans to go to dinner and a movie.

Finally, signs that your nest is evolving also involves places. Somewhere other than *your* nest will now serve as a temporary home for your young adult. A bedroom in your home becomes empty as a room somewhere else now holds your young adult's clothes and clutter. As your son or daughter begins to explore new surroundings, treat yourself to some discoveries as well. Make believe you're a tourist in your hometown and take it in with a fresh perspective.

The Shift—your Shift—is the emotional and physical experience of all those changes in your nest, as well as the aftermath of the changes. Refeathering the nest is the journey that lies ahead. As you peer into the future, imagine the tangible evidence of events, people, and places that hold fulfillment and satisfaction for you as a person, not just you as a parent.

2

STAGES OF THE SHIFT

Getting over a painful experience is much like crossing monkey bars. You have to let go at some point in order to move forward.

—C. S. Lewis, novelist and poet

Life's milestones are often captured in terms of "firsts" and "lasts"—first words, last day of high school, first child, last breath. Prior to baby boomers, it was somewhat easier than it is now to designate phases of life by identifying the milestones that framed them. For many in the World War II generation, for example, the period between freshman and senior years of high school might be characterized as their "young adult" phase, with military service or jobs marking the beginning of their adulthood. By the time baby boomers were growing up, the shape of the life cycle had already started to change dramatically, with young adulthood more likely spanning the end of high school and continuing through the early to mid-twenties. As a corollary, the phases of life became less delineated. This is certainly true for the Shift.

In fact, it is no longer meaningful to consider the "empty nest" a milestone, since the experience of having one's children move toward independence and autonomy is not a single event, but rather a series of events. The Shift is fluid.

While there are benchmarks and signs to identify which stage of the Shift a parent is experiencing—anticipation, launching, or resolution—the stages can be unique to the individual. However, the one common experience is in the launching stage, when the young adult departs toward an independent life. This departure is the milestone event of the Shift.

This moment of the Shift can be a profound experience for both an individual parent and a parenting couple, who might feel a sense of loss when their child moves away. Elisabeth Kübler-Ross's work on how people respond to loss in the context of death offers insight that is useful for people experiencing other types of losses. She categorizes responses into the following five stages: denial, anger, bargaining, depression, and acceptance.[1] In so doing, she captures what many parents go through in the stages of the Shift. But whereas Kübler-Ross primarily addresses how people may act in the face of physical death, in the Shift, the central event is the parents' loss of their child's dependence on them, with increased absence from their lives. At the same time, they sense a loss of significance in their child's life; they no longer have the ability to regulate and influence what happens to the child. Both the child's dependence and the sense of significance as a parent reflect a whole world of interconnectedness in terms of school, extracurricular activities, social events, and future plans. For years, day after day, parents go through gyrations—for example, editing their children's papers, assisting them with college applications, and cheering them on during competitions. With the child moving out, they experience not only the loss of the child's presence in the home, but also the loss of an intense focus on parenting and involvement in their child's life.

In terms of parenting, the first generation of parents launching their children into adulthood in the twenty-first century is different from the ones that went before. They do, however, give a good indication of what the trend is for the foreseeable future. Research indicates that putting career first and marriage and children later has impacted the parenting style of many couples.[2] Many of these parents have immersed themselves in parenting as though it were a career—in the most positive and passionate sense. In other words, they may not see parenting as just work—that is, something expected by society—but rather a commitment they carefully choose to fulfill in an informed and educated way.

So when the children leave the nest, the life they knew while rearing their children is dramatically transformed. It's as though life hands them a new job description, and they are asked to change as the environment changes. Parents with full-time careers can feel it, because the need to weigh and juggle priorities between work and home shrinks or disappears. The stay-at-home parent may feel this change even more acutely, regardless of whether or not she combined parenting with a home-based career and/or a vigorous schedule of volunteering.

One common question that arises is this: What am I going to do to fill in the space, the holes, the time that used to go to the range of parenting activities that included staying closely attuned to the child's trials and tribulations? That question can elicit a variety of feelings: fear, excitement, sadness, and uncertainty, to name just a few. The holes that arise in a parent's daily experiences may be experienced as gaps—at least at first. However, gaps can become portals through which loss becomes opportunity. That transition in perception from loss to opportunity is something that hopefully happens in the Shift, generally in the final stage of resolution.

When parents finally see the portal take shape, that doesn't mean they stop missing having their children at home and those daily activities that were part of parenting. They notice the difference in daily life from having them gone and how their life has reformed. Like a yard that changes with the seasons, the landscape looks different.

The Shift is both personal and interpersonal. Often it triggers parents to evaluate their most important relationships, particularly the intimate ones. First of all, they have more time for the relationship with themselves. They also have more opportunity to consider thoughtfully the relationships they have with their spouse, their own parents, in-laws, and friends. The impact of this is discussed in more detail in Part II.

OVERVIEW OF THE STAGES

It might be useful to envision the Shift as beginning with subtle indicators of what is about to come, followed by the potentially disorienting reality of it, and then a sense of moving toward solid ground.

Anticipation

Anticipation is palpable, even though many of the signs of it are subtle. The earliest hints might be something like passing the child's empty room when she's off at summer camp; it's a preview of what it will be like to have the young adult vacate the room on a more permanent basis. Another subtle reminder, closer to the actual event of the young adult's departure, is the high school calendar mentioned in chapter 1. Many of the signs of anticipation relate to preparation—getting a driver's license, dating, holding down the first part-time job, taking standardized tests, filling out applications for college or trade school—so this phase can last for years. When President Barack Obama talked about his daughters being noticeably absent from the home more often when Sasha and Malia were just twelve and fifteen years old, respectively, he was expressing a common sentiment of parents who are in the initial stage of the Shift.

In the interviews I conducted to collect stories and insights for this book, I always asked the parents when they first felt a sense of anticipation about the Shift. Most responses were consistent with the above, but one stood out as an example of humorous exaggeration: "When our oldest son was born and we were bringing him home in the car I started crying. My husband asked me, 'Why are you crying?' I said, 'He's going to college!'"

Regardless of exactly when the young adult moves on toward independence, there is still an anticipation phase. A parenting group that I facilitate for mothers of elementary school children consists of women who are all about ten years away from having their children move out of the home. They sometimes talk long-ingly about the day when their children will be on their own and they'll have more time and space to do things they can't usually do now. But even in the middle of saying, "I can't wait!" they also share precious and memorable moments about their children. They convey the sense of wanting to freeze-dry those special mo-ments, attempting to preserve them forever. These feelings are the precursor of the Shift. They reflect awareness that these won-derful moments are time-limited. As arduous as the day-to-day trials of growing up are, this is a magical time and they acknowl-edge they will miss it someday.

But it's generally in the high school years, especially the junior and senior years, that the anticipation stage becomes more pro-nounced. As it does, stress becomes evident and it can surface in discussions between parents and their emerging young adults.

A common dynamic experienced by parents—and their chil-dren—as they enter the anticipation stage of the Shift is a push-pull phenomenon. Both parent and child have a struggle in finding the balance between when "mommy" can help and when "mother" needs to back off. One day the young adult wants his parents to take care of him and do everything, and the next day he wants to be independent and not reliant on parents at all. This dynamic is discussed at length and with humor by clinical psychologist Antho-ny Wolf in his book *Get out of My Life, but First Could You Drive Me and Cheryl to the Mall?*.

The push-pull conflict is not only common, it is also *necessary*, just as when the child first tried to exercise some control and self-reliance as a toddler. The job of two-year-olds is to begin to ex-press independence. Psychoanalyst Erik Erickson, well-known for his eight-stage theory of identity and psychosocial development,[3] describes this as a time when children have an opportunity to build self-esteem and autonomy in the process of learning new skills. When parents support that process, children become sure of themselves and proudly take credit for everything they do. They want to walk by themselves, but still need adult help. It's necessary for parents to go from holding two hands, to one, and, ultimately, to give just a pinky to toddlers to give them the confidence and skill set to be able to walk. It's also necessary for parents to allow them to fall. They help their children by letting them get bumps and bruises. When children are that age, the parents may feel a sense of accomplishment and pride because they provided support when it was needed and backed off when it wasn't.

Parenting college-age young adults has a lot of parallels. The young adults will learn a great deal about how to make good decisions by making bad decisions and it's important for parents to let them earn those bumps and bruises. In short, the same skill set parents used when helping toddlers through the terrible twos comes into play again when the children are leaving home. When launching children into adult independence, however, that skill set matures and involves new levels of complexity.

Launching

Launching is evidenced by events. Unlike anticipation, this stage is not marked by subtleties. Specific events occur that force parents to focus on the reality of major life changes. They may feel a void in the pit of the stomach, a sense of emptiness and fear, along with other emotions. For about eighteen years, they've invested heavily in creating a status quo that has suddenly imploded—at least that's how abrupt and dramatic it can feel.

In talking with many baby boomers who are now going through the Shift, a common scenario emerged. Their own experience of leaving home differed greatly from what twenty-first century young adults are encountering. Results from the national survey conducted in support of this book indicated that more than two-thirds of the respondents considered their young adults' experience of leaving home either dissimilar or opposite from their own. Baby boomers' parents commonly put them on a plane or a bus with luggage and then they moved onto campus alone. In other cases, parents drove them to the campus, helped get the luggage to the room, and then left.

The prevailing perception of launching at that time was that it was an inevitable culmination of raising children and that parents would experience it and move on through middle age. It was perceived as a milestone in life. The event of launching and related adjustments would occur automatically, according to a team of sociologists who co-authored a mid-1980s journal article aptly named "Launching Children and Moving On." A 1973 study covered in the journal *Family Process* also described how the launch was viewed at that time—that is, there was a high degree of predictability in the way parents transitioned from finding gratification in raising children to finding gratification in ways that were unrelated to their role as parents.[4] The strong sense of causality that dominated traditional thinking about the launch had mainstream acceptance: When children grew up, then they moved out of the nest; when they moved out of the nest, then parents moved into the next phase of their lives.

In contrast, the Shift is not characterized by predictability. The experience of this life phase differs from person to person and family to family. One difference that is quite apparent is that today's parents are much more likely to have continued involvement in their young adult's life. Whereas the parents of baby boomers commonly dropped them off at the dorm, today's parents invest the time to help them move into their dorm or first apartment. With Lysol in hand to sanitize the room, hangers and shoe bags to organize the clothes, and maybe a few favorite items from their bedroom at home, parents attempt to maintain a sense of hearth and home as it was before the child's departure. For some parents, it may be an unconscious attempt to maintain some semblance of a familiar nest—like adhering to an outdated job description. Carrying over that status quo seems natural.

Resolution

Resolution can occur so subtly that parents can be well into it before they realize they've entered a defining moment of the

Shift. The mother no longer even thinks of buying her daughter's favorite cereal when she's at the store. The father has been playing golf with a neighbor on Sunday mornings; he's stopped flashing back to the time when the set of clubs next to his in the car belonged to his teenage son.

Returning to the metaphor of the landscape, at some point, the parent or parenting couple sees the new growth in the yard. It doesn't happen overnight, but it's an inescapable and necessary change. This sense of resolution and optimism that occurs after all young adults are finally out of the house went virtually unrecognized in professional literature until the baby boomer generation experienced it.

When researchers first started using the phrase "empty nest syndrome" in 1966,[5] their reference points and study participants were different even from those of Gail Sheehy, who wrote *Passages* a mere ten years later. When the phrase first became part of psychology literature, the research focused on the depression and sense of isolation some people felt when their young adults left home. Many, if not most, of the other parents in their generation arrived at "the marker" (to use Sheehy's term) and then moved on; a few others experienced this newly codified "syndrome." As suggested by the literature of the 1970s and 1980s cited in the launching discussion, having difficulty after the launch was not at all considered typical.

Studies prior to the twenty-first century seemed to center primarily on those parents, specifically mothers, who felt they were not coping well with an empty nest. In contrast, in this century we are seeing a proliferation of studies giving a complete picture of the process: anticipating the young adult moving out, launching the young adult, and then adjusting to the aftermath in what I call the resolution stage of the Shift. As a result, we are seeing articles such as "Empty Nest Syndrome May Not Be Bad After All."[6] In short, there seems to be an increased attention on the whole spectrum of cognitive and emotional responses to having our young adults leave the home.

OVERVIEW OF RESPONSES TO THE STAGES

In first considering how people respond to anticipation and launching, I thought about different animals and how they might represent the different ways people experience the Shift. I introduced the concept earlier and want to revisit it here because these iconic symbols have helped many people I've talked with about the Shift. The hummingbird darts frenetically from place to place. The parents who become the hummingbirds keep themselves so busy that they do not stay in one place, doing one thing, for very long. It could be busy work, or it could be an intense flurry of volunteer or career activity. They unconsciously avoid feeling the impending change by having such a hectic life; they don't give themselves the time or space to feel.

For example, Cindy's passion was being a mother to her two boys. As many parents do, she took enormous pride in the fact that she had documented their lives in photographs, which were placed perfectly in dozens of picture frames throughout the house. Her life revolved around her children, both of whom were star athletes. She never missed one of her older son's soccer games or her younger son's wrestling matches. When Cindy's older son left for college, she began substitute teaching. Three years later, when her younger son was a junior in high school, she started taking courses toward her master's degree in education. By the time he graduated from high school and left for college, she was up to two courses a semester, a full-time job, and taking yoga on Saturdays. She also sang in the church choir. Even with all those activities, she kept trying to do more, as though she wanted every minute of her life filled. It's no coincidence that within six months of her son's leaving, Cindy and her husband filed for divorce. Much of Cindy's gratification in life had come from parenting. In trying to fill the void when she was no longer needed daily as a parent, she found many things to do, but none of them included additional focus on her marriage.

Then there is the stunned deer. This person is so frightened, and even shocked, that she doesn't know what to do. For years, her steps are predictable: go to the PTA meeting, attend the game, pick the children up after school. After the youngest child leaves for college, she becomes a stunned deer. With no plan for her next step, she remains still, frozen in one place, doing nothing toward evolving the nest.

Elizabeth was so child-centered throughout the time she raised her daughter that she had no idea where to start when her only child left home. She was bewildered and really didn't know which way to turn to restore some structure to her life. The spectrum of possibilities around her, like volunteering or working part-time, seemed overwhelming. Not knowing how to find fulfillment in her day, she simply stood still, like the deer in the middle of the street with cars whizzing by on both sides. She longed for the days when she watched her daughter in ballet class, went shopping with her on Saturdays, and baked cookies with her during the holidays. Those days were gone, but she couldn't get them out of her thoughts, so she remained stuck. With the help of a support group, she discovered she was unable to see her options. Her family and friends helped her take the next steps—figuratively helping her cross the street—by encouraging her to get involved with something she enjoyed. Her first step was playing the piano twice a week for a Level 1 ballet class at the school her daughter had attended.

The stunned deer is a temporary state, just as the others are. Elizabeth regained her energy for daily activities and enthusiasm for her marriage and home. She began volunteering at the local hospital, which renewed her interest in the nursing career she had left behind when she became pregnant with her daughter. Her husband and friends encouraged her every step of the way, caring for her in a manner that helped her "cross the highway."

Another animal type is the eager beaver, who reads everything about the subject and does everything possible to manage his feelings. The eager beaver responds to the Shift by making it a profession, just as he had made parenting a career, full of passion, persistence, and a strong sense of priorities.

Keith appreciated how much his wife, a stay-at-home mom, had always been there for their only child, a son. When their son reached his junior year of high school, Keith made a concerted effort to help with college preparation. He created checklists, folders of critical information comparing colleges, schedules indicating what needed to be done in the months before college—all prepared with professional excellence. Nothing was left to chance. After his son was gone, he continued to be constructive and busy; it helped quiet the feelings he had about his only son leaving home. He focused on the home: There were checklists for every social event, labels on all the boxes in the garage, and plans for vacations he wanted to take with his wife for the next ten years. Eventually, as he adjusted to life without his son at home, his need for organizing decreased, and he no longer needed to keep himself busy to ward off his feelings. Keith redirected his focus to his marriage and the many years he and his wife would hopefully have together.

Keep in mind that these categories are fluid. The most likely scenario is that people are not consistently one way or another, but rather move from one category to another. It's possible to get a glimpse of the categories where survey respondents fit based on their descriptions of how they use the extra time they now have. Catching up on projects at work and volunteering were two common ways they used the time, both of which suggest focused activities and a sense of productivity. However, 23 percent indicated they were "keeping busy in a random way." This may suggest they are uncertain about the direction their life is heading or how they hope to reshape their life. They may be exploring different options as a way to zero in on what they want in this next stage.

Responding to Anticipation

Anticipation tends to be a protracted stage of the Shift, so responding with denial makes a great deal of sense. Not wanting to let go is normal. To quote from Kübler-Ross about denial, "I regard it as a healthy way of dealing with the uncomfortable and painful situation with which some of these (people) have to live for a very long time." She goes on to say that denial allows a person "to collect himself and, with time, mobilize other, less radical, defenses."[7]

It can go to extremes, though. The "failure to launch" circumstance described in the 2006 movie of the same name, with Matthew McConaughey portraying an adult living comfortably with his parents and Sarah Jessica Parker as the woman hired to incite his interest in moving out, has its roots in denial. Parents send a mixed message: They want the young adult to grow up, but are scared for him to move on and of feeling unneeded. As a consequence, they are unable to set limits on what happens in the home, thereby creating an environment where the young adult finds it desirable to remain a child in some day-to-day ways.

Anger and the spectrum of related emotions, such as annoyance and exasperation, can be an unconscious way parents push their children away. For example, a parent might nag the young adult about his hair and style of dress even though he hasn't changed anything about his appearance in months. It's not a deliberate act to push the young adult away, but this unconscious expression of emotion does contribute to the dynamic that keeps the young adult moving toward independence. Conversely, children might push their parents away by doing things unconsciously that provoke their parents, such as keeping their room messy or being late for curfew.

Turning to Kübler-Ross again for insights on how anger works, we might categorize it as a much more stress-provoking response than denial. Anger is a more identifiable emotion that's expressed by being late, criticizing, nagging, leaving clothes draped over chairs, and so on. In contrast, denial reflects avoidance; an internal barrier goes up and retains emotions behind it. Also, anger can be "displaced in all directions and projected onto the environment at times almost at random,"[8] according to Kübler-Ross. In other words, it can be projected onto other people who happen to be in the vicinity and may not have anything to do with the situation at home. For example, a parent having some anger about the youngest child leaving might blow up at his boss over a routine request.

When the young adult projects this kind of emotion, the source could be anxiety over leaving home that plays out as exasperation over various things the parents are doing to prepare for the move. The same thing holds true for the parents, who might get annoyed with the young adult over inconsequential things largely because they may be feeling apprehension of the unknown.

Among the five stages of loss identified by Kübler-Ross—denial, anger, bargaining, depression, and acceptance—bargaining may involve the most creativity; that is, it may give rise to some very inventive approaches for a parent to get what he or she wants. And as stated at the beginning of the chapter, these responses are not necessarily discrete; they may overlap, so a parent might be bargaining while experiencing denial, for example.

When parents engage in bargaining, it tends to be a conscious and deliberate negotiation. They want a particular outcome with their young adult and hope that they can create a set of circumstances whereby they get it. They may lose sight of the fact that bargaining generally does not yield a sustainable solution. I know one set of parents who told their daughter they would buy her a car if she would go through at least freshman year at a college within a half hour of her home—so she could continue to live at home for another year—instead of attending a college eight hours away.

If we slightly stretch the concept of bargaining, it's also possible to envision a less premeditated variation. For example, mom might text, "I'm making your favorite meal tonight!" to her high school senior on a Friday afternoon. It could have the effect of keeping him at home for a couple of hours instead of rushing off to get together with buddies right after school. Even though mom hadn't calculated that outcome, hindsight might make her conscious of the fact that "favorite meal" might be a good bargaining chip in the future. Other bargaining actions might be doing laundry weekly or buying clothes periodically. All of these actions engender the young adult's dependence on the parent, while the parents maintain more contact with the young adult than they would if they didn't do these things.

A fourth response to anticipation is sadness. If a parent feels dejected in this stage of the Shift, even some of the time, it may be for any number of reasons: a diminished sense of self-worth, loss of control over the child's life, or perhaps regrets over "not doing enough" as a parent. If the degree of sadness impacts daily life, it may be useful to seek professional advice.

Responding to Launching

When the young adult comes back home for a visit, it's common for parent and child to revert back to the patterns that elicit annoyance, dependence, and other states associated with the push-pull dynamic. Tension can get ratcheted up to the point of anger quite easily. Often, the young adult regresses simply because he's back in the parents' home again. In his absence, however, the parents have become accustomed to a neat and clean room. The young adult doesn't respond to suggestions of "clean up the room" because he has become used to having control over his living space; he no longer wants anyone managing him. In fact, the young adult may unconsciously rebel by being even more careless than usual. Regardless of the impetus, it can provoke anger, or at least annoyance.

There is also frustration, and possibly anger, that plays out between the couple when one spouse experiences the launch acutely, while the other one does not because fewer elements of his daily routine have been altered. "You don't understand how *I* feel!" might be how one spouse accuses another of not being in touch with a sense of loss of day-to-day parenting. One person's routine is completely disrupted by the departure of the child, while the other person continues to go to work at 7:30 a.m., participate in meetings, have lunch with clients, and come home around 7:30 p.m. This is one of the many couple-related issues addressed in chapter 4.

Parents of both genders maintain a keen sense of continuity by focusing on parenting activities on a day-to-day basis, regardless of the different routines they may have. That said, it is normal for mothers, whether they are working outside the home or not, to have a greater sense of awareness to the ongoing requirements of children. Neuropsychiatrist Louann Brizendine attributes this reality to what she calls the "mommy brain": "Motherhood changes you because it literally alters a woman's brain—structurally, functionally, and in many ways, irreversibly. It's nature's way, you could say, of ensuring the survival of the species."[9]

A parent going through launching might also feel depression. There is a sense of sadness and loss related to no longer parenting in a way that had been ongoing, habitual, comfortable, and expected. Not feeling needed in the same way, or not feeling needed at all, is a common reason for feeling sad. A spouse, partner, or others in a person's life might evoke the sadness and cause her to wonder: "Am I less than the person I used to be?" "Do you love me for who I am without the children around?" In *Counterclockwise: Mindful Health and the Power of Possibility*, psychologist Ellen Langer points out how much people around us can impact such feelings. She notes that cues in our environment prime how we feel, and that those feelings change from moment to moment.[10]

On the other hand, the sadness may be relieved by responses from spouses, partners, or friends. They may serve as a source of reassurance and may cause her to question the validity of her feelings. In the context of a couple, it may involve a growing realization that, with parenting not being front and center in their lives, they have more time for each other. They can get back to where they were when they first got together. Again, this is an issue explored more thoroughly in chapter 4.

For some people, sadness means missing elements of life they enjoyed greatly, such as the company of one's children and the good times they shared. Actress Alfre Woodard, whose credits include the movie *Primal Fear* and the television show *Desperate Housewives*, talked about how she felt when her youngest left home: "I'm three weeks into my empty nest and I'm still a little weepy."[11] As busy as Woodward was making a new TV movie, she had the kind of normal sadness that many parents share shortly after the youngest has departed.

Responding to Resolution

Readers familiar with Elisabeth Kübler-Ross's work might think of resolution as equivalent to "acceptance." In the Shift, acceptance would be an element of resolution, but the two are not synonymous concepts. In the context of Kübler-Ross's discussion of death and dying, acceptance is a cognitive process, not an emotional one.[12] In contrast to that, I want to make the distinction that the resolution stage of the Shift can be filled with emotions, although underlying them is acknowledgment that the inevitable has occurred. That acknowledgment might be described as "acceptance" in the Kübler-Ross sense.

Once parents have entered the resolution stage of the Shift, they hopefully have a sense of moving on and renewal. This would be similar to people who respond to retirement with a focus on opportunities—the prospect of being able to travel or play golf during the week excites them. For others, however, retirement is daunting. The thought of having unplanned days or the sense of not being needed might frighten them. A desire to hang on to the past might dominate their thoughts and actions. After launching their young adult, parents could have analogous responses to that person who initially faces retirement with fear or a sense of being stuck. In short, myriad responses, potentially leading to changes in interpersonal relationships, are likely to take shape.

When her young adults were ages twenty and twenty-three, actress Kyra Sedgwick (*The Closer*) described her emotional transition from launch to resolution in a way that many of us can relate to:

> I think I grieved an entire year over the process, and I still get boo-hooey sometimes, but I'm so grateful that they're still talk-

ing to me and they want me to be part of their lives. I do miss that level of need and intimacy we once had. As a parent, you have such a great job, and you feel like you're pretty good at it—then you kinda get fired. But it's also the exact right nature of things, and I take solace in that.[13]

In part II, I look at how the responses to different stages of the Shift affect the individual, intimate relationships with others, and perceptions of one's success or regrets as a parent.

THOUGHTS TO CONSIDER

The three stages of the Shift—anticipation, launching, and resolution—defy sharp delineation. Anticipation of the launch, as some of the contributors to this book humorously pointed out, can fleetingly enter your thoughts right after the birth of your child. In a practical and meaningful sense, however, it begins when palpable changes occur prior to the youngest child leaving the nest. The actual departure of that young adult is certainly a clear marker; nonetheless, even the launching stage cannot be reduced to a single moment in time. It involves a process of making lists, packing bags, loading the car, putting neatly folded clothes in dormitory drawers, and so on. Resolution is the leg of the journey that probably varies most from person to person. Embracing your life after day-to-day parenting happens quickly for some, while for others it can take a while.

Given that these stages, taken together, generally encompass years, there is ample opportunity to experience a spectrum of responses to them. In this chapter, I introduced some of these responses through references to three iconic images: the hummingbird, stunned deer, and eager beaver. You may find yourself identifying with all of them at different times of the Shift.

If you find yourself frenetically moving like the hummingbird—every waking moment is busy—your objective is to slow down. That's easier said than done if you feel overwhelmed with the details of your young adult's imminent departure, for example, or overcome by the need to feel just as productive as you were when your parenting skills were required daily.

This is a time when making a list can help. Write down everything you believe you need to do and rank each entry in terms of priority. At the same time, ask yourself an important question: Is your hummingbird behavior different from other behavior you've had in the past when you have experienced significant change in your life? If you recognize it as something familiar, then perhaps it's a default response. Think back to your first days in college, getting married, having your first child. You may realize that hummingbird behavior is part of your temporary coping strategy. Just knowing that may help you to quell the frenetic reaction to the demands and changes going on in your nest.

On the other hand, if you don't remember acting like this before, be kind to yourself. Parenting has been your focus for many years and the unknowns you now face with grown children may spark reactions you've never had before. Again, just knowing that may help you slow down a bit.

For the stunned deer, it's very helpful to take a look at what is on either side of the road. You need to know which way to move to lessen the sense of being overwhelmed. In this situation, explore sets of options. If you moved one way, what would the outcome be? If you moved the other, what would the outcome be? And is there a third or a fourth direction to move?

The alternate paths might involve your relationship with your spouse or young adult, your aspirations to launch a new career, or any number of other parts of your life. The important thing is to identify these paths, and then weigh and measure each set of possibilities so you can make a more confident and sound decision as you proceed. If you find yourself being indecisive, rely on your intuition and simply move.

From the outside looking in, eager beavers appear to have their act together. They've made the launch of their young adult a profession. Eager beavers, however, may work so hard to be proficient at managing the demands of launching that they don't allow themselves space and time to go through associated feelings.

If you find this describes you some of the time, consider that no beaver can make sure every stick and log is in the right place in the dam. There are always unpredictable factors, so go easy on yourself. For everyone going through the Shift, there is a learning curve.

As I highlighted in the discussion of the hummingbird, you may have a default response to significant changes, unknowns, and challenges. That also holds true if you find yourself behaving like the stunned deer or eager beaver. It is also true that you may find yourself acting in ways that seem foreign to you. Having your children leave your home is a major change and there is no way to predict how it will affect you. So take comfort in knowing that these feelings, which seem abnormal, are common and natural.

2

Realities of the Shift

3

THE ROLE OF PERSONAL EXPERIENCE

When mothers talk about the depression of the empty nest, they're not mourning the passing of all those wet towels on the floor, or the music that numbs your teeth, or even the bottle of capless shampoo dribbling down the shower drain. They're upset because they've gone from supervisor of a child's life to a spectator. It's like being the vice president of the United States.

—Erma Bombeck, author and humorist

"Mommy!"

Every time she heard a child sob, scream, or say the word with delight, Suzie would turn around. She had exchanged her nursing career for a career as a stay-at-home mom for her three children. Her identity had become primarily "mommy" and she embraced it wholeheartedly. She vividly remembers responding to all shouts of "mommy!" when her children were growing up, and hearing from her friends that they shared that experience. Even after her youngest child was in her last year of college, Suzie continued to turn around when she heard it. She couldn't seem to tone down the "mommy" persona.

One evening she was at the movies with her husband of twenty-four years and she heard a child yell "the word." She craned her neck to see where the distraught child was. Her husband laughed and said, "Suzie, you are not mommy to every child on earth!" His teasing caused her to wonder if it might be time to cultivate the other dimensions of her identity. "I'll probably always instinctively turn around when I hear a child call 'mommy,'" Suzie concluded, "but I want to continue to be a wife, a Red Cross volunteer, and so much more, in addition to being the mother of three wonderful girls."

With the departure, or imminent departure, of young adults from the home, it's natural for parents to wonder, "Who am I other than a parent?" And for all the reasons mentioned earlier in the book, the more common scenario is for the woman to wonder "Who am I other than a mommy/mother?" The question may not ever be voiced. It may just rumble around inside one's head and intensify the emotions related to the Shift. The question itself doesn't necessarily cause pain. Ideally, it initiates a process of discovery, which may evoke some unsettling thoughts and emotions, and it may give rise to some equally happy ones as well.

FALLACY OF THE SYNDROME

Defining a stage of life as "empty nest" is a set up for thinking of it as negative. Add the word "syndrome" after the phrase, and it suddenly implies that a natural life experience somehow engenders disease.

Pairing "syndrome" with "empty nest" conveys an inaccuracy. The Mayo Clinic website states: "Empty nest syndrome isn't a clinical diagnosis."[1] In other words, it is not a mental or physical illness. The casual and common use of the phrase "empty nest syndrome" in our society works against parents who are experiencing an important phase of life—one that should not be put in the same category as a disease.

For that reason, it is my intent to stay away from using the phrase as much as possible. The nest is not empty. Even after children leave, the nest is still a home; it just may need to be refeathered. (One way to think of it is remodeling.)

Michelle Duggar, mother of nineteen children, serves as an extreme example of someone who aims to avoid the feelings associated with having young adult children leave home. During an August 24, 2012 interview on the *Today* show, she said, "I think that it will be a sad day for me whenever I know that we're not able to have any more [children]. . . . Hopefully, we won't have that empty nest syndrome." Reinforcing how serious she and her husband, Jim Bob, are about avoiding that situation, they stated in a March 2013 interview with *People Magazine* that they were considering either adopting another child or having another child—or more.

A key theme woven throughout this book is the benefit of reshaping the concept of empty nest into "evolving nest." As stated above, the nest is not empty: it's different. By definition "different" isn't positive or negative. Practically speaking, "different" may upset some people. A professor once told me she had observed that an astonishingly high percentage of students occupied the same spot in the lecture hall, or very close to the same spot, throughout a semester. Given hundreds of seats to choose from, they claimed "their" spot. This story illustrates the fact that people automatically do things that are familiar, without thinking. There is a sense of comfort and reassurance without change. With change, or "different," comes the Goldilocks challenge alluded to in chapter 1: You don't want to end up with something too hard or too soft.

In order to explore a range of responses to the Shift, I conducted multiple, web-based surveys with parents of young adults in the United States. One of the questions asked them to express what their *first* reaction was to launching their young adult, as follows:

My first feeling about my child leaving home was probably:

Anxiety	43%
Depression	7%

Anger	0%
Fear	17%
Excitement	33%

In terms of gender, 47 percent of the respondents were female and 53 percent were male. The percentage of men who volunteered to take the survey speaks volumes about societal changes as they relate to parenting from the 1950s and 1960s to the new millennium. It was atypical for fathers in the World War II generation and prior to that to be involved in virtually all aspects of parenting. Today, however, many men have a shared experience of Precision Parenting with their partners and have something to say about their feelings when the youngest child leaves home. The fact that their lives no longer encompass the schedule of games, parent-teacher meetings, and other events on the high school calendar can be a jarring change to them. Beginning with the baby boomer generation, parenting has touched men and women in a way it never had before.

Consistent with this change, an increasing number of articles about the "empty nest" are written by men. In addition, the increased male participation in the day-to-day activities of parenting is widely noted. For example, syndicated columnist Sarah Smiley is the daughter of a career Navy officer and is married to a Navy pilot. In a 2013 article about how the challenges of changing gender roles are affecting military fathers, she notes that her husband was noticeably absent from the activities that other dads routinely participated in, whereas when she was growing up, her father's absence was not as obvious:

> I looked around at a baseball game and noticed how many fathers were there. Some of them had left work early and were still in their business suits. Dads were at the parent-teacher conferences at school, too. Indeed, they seemed to be everywhere we moms were.[2]

While many fathers in nonmilitary careers have demands that also keep them away, of course, her central point is an important one: It has become common for fathers to rearrange their schedules to participate more fully in the lives of their children.

A study conducted by researchers at Wellesley College and published in the *Journal of Marriage and the Family* documented that fatherhood impacts the physical and mental health of many men in this modern age just as much as their careers.[3] In *New Passages*, Gail Sheehy refers to these men as "new-model fathers" and she notes:

> These daddies are different. They are discovering a secret that women have always known: The easiest way to feel loved and needed and ten feet tall is to be an involved parent.[4]

To bring that thought into the context of the Shift, once a father gets involved and stays involved in parenting, it is inevitable that he will have strong emotional responses to the departure of children from the nest. Included in this group of involved fathers are some who already raised one family as a relatively uninvolved parent, and then plunged into fatherhood intensely when they decided to start a second family. These "start-over dads" are likely to experience the Shift as well, even though they have already gone through the experience of launching children. The level of involvement is a key determinant in the emotional response a parent has to the departure of children from the home.

Collectively, male and female respondents described their parenting style in the top three categories in terms of level of involvement, as follows:

How would you describe your parenting style?

I am extremely involved in my   22%
child's life.

I pay attention to my child's life   49%
and am involved quite a bit.

I try to know what's going on in my child's life, but give him/her a lot of space.	28%
I wait for my child to involve me in his/her life.	0%
My child is very independent.	1%

Any of the emotions identified in the surveys can carry different meanings depending on the person. One parent might be anxious about a child adjusting to new surroundings, whereas another might be anxious about having so much free time. And even though no one chose "anger" as a first emotional response, many stories collected for this project indicate it is very much a part of the spectrum of emotions felt by a parent who has just launched a young adult. And just as anxiety or excitement can have different meanings, so can anger.

Anger commonly rises up in a flash and disappears just as quickly, unlike some of the other emotions that persist for days or months. For example, a parent might lash out at a spouse for not participating enough in college preparation with an accusation like, "I did everything to get him ready for college and you did nothing!" Moments later, those words might be followed by an apology: "I'm sorry; I don't know why I said that." Momentary anger might also be directed at the young adult, who forgot to call during spring break or has decided to spend part of his winter break going skiing instead of being at home.

STORIES OF INITIAL RESPONSES

Anxiety

A parent's concern for a young adult's vulnerabilities can be one cause of anxiety. Perhaps the teenager had been a little out of the loop socially, or had some difficulty academically. There are many reasons for wondering if the young adult can succeed in a new and unfamiliar environment and be independent. Some parents may worry about their own ability to adjust to changes in the nest and how it may impact their life.

When preparing for her daughter to leave for college, Sally arranged for her to meet a number of other people in the area who were going to the same school. In addition to helping her daughter through the transition, she was helping herself feel more comfortable with it. Sally created a sense of familiarity about the new environment that was reassuring to both of them. It gave Sally a chance to meet some of the people who would be in the same setting as her daughter, as well as establish camaraderie with the parents of those young adults.

Sometimes, the anxiety comes from recognizing that the youngest child's departure spotlights a crossroads. One of the women I interviewed reflected on her mother's illness and passing as part of her experience of launching her child. As Leigh had seen her mother get sicker over a period of months, she began to think about the choices she had made, primarily the decision to remain married to someone who had consistently been a source of stress. Faced with the reality of soon having no more children at home—of essentially being alone with a man she found unresponsive and difficult—she grappled with tremendous anxiety. She wondered how both her husband and children would feel if she initiated a divorce, and questioned whether she would feel a disconnection from friends she had made in her community. She had watched her mother stay in a dysfunctional marriage that appeared to the outside world to be a "normal" union. Her anxiety over her own situation was fueled by her internal conflict: Follow in her mother's footsteps or try to change the outcome.

Depression

A sense of being alone or of not being understood by a spouse or partner could easily trigger some level of depression.

Anne was a stay-at-home mom who had a houseful of children's noise, laundry, and friends for nearly thirty years. She found the new circumstances of silence, lack of clutter, and emptiness an unbearable change—unbearable because it signaled a lack of purpose in life. In contrast to her life after the children left, her husband continued his thriving practice as an orthopedic surgeon. He rose at dawn and headed for the hospital for morning surgeries. She lingered in bed, not feeling the slightest motivation to get out and do anything. No one *expected* her to do anything anymore, she thought, and most of her adult life had been shaped by expectations—of getting meals ready on time, helping with homework, and giving hugs to take away the pain of a skinned knee. The loss of routine in addition to a diminished sense of purpose contributed to a downward spiral for Anne that became depression.

Psychologist Deborah Rozman, author of *Transforming Depression*, compares the type of depression mothers might feel after launching a child to the kind some experience after birth:

> Empty-nesters can experience a unique kind of post-partum depression. Having this kind of time is a luxury for some, a relief for others, and still, for some, a terrifying void to fill. How do you relate to your spouse without your child as the main focus? . . . What's going to nurture you? What's your heart's purpose now? What's the next level of fulfillment in your life?[5]

Rozman offers a number of thoughts for parents who feel depressed over what they perceive as the loss of a child, and with it, a sense of purpose and direction. The most important thing to note is that one may experience a sense of depression as part of the journey through the Shift. If it becomes chronic, then professional help may be warranted; however, it often lessens over time. Finding a level of fulfillment in your life that helps you move through depression has no formula. There is no systematic program that's guaranteed to counter the sense of loss you might feel over having your children move out of the home.

Anger

One response to having children out of the house can be the investment of even more time in career. And because the departure of young adults generally comes at a time when a career may be cresting, a person may feel a sense of urgency to work as hard as possible—perhaps to "cash in"—before retirement. For the spouse or partner whose career was raising children, seeing the only other person living in the home pay more attention to work than the marriage could arouse a lot of resentment and anger.

At the same time, the husband may be perplexed at the negative emotions the wife is displaying. He might then return the anger: "You should realize that I have to do this now so we have something to live on later!" She may experience his response as dismissive and lacking understanding of what she is going through. Tensions could escalate, with his reactions likely to exacerbate her anger and frustration.

That same kind of disconnect can apply to the parent's relationship with the young adult who is moving out, as the following story illustrates.

Jane was an environmental consultant for sixteen years before she married at the age of thirty-six and became a stay-at-home mom at age thirty-eight. She was close to her two daughters and very involved in their lives, serving as everything from PTA president to the go-to mom for supervising field trips.

Jane and her youngest daughter had agreed to spend time together packing suitcases and then loading the car the night before her daughter was scheduled to leave for college. Instead, when her daughter received a phone call from a high school friend inviting her to a party, she abruptly left and said she'd see her later. Jane felt hurt over feeling secondary in importance to her daughter's friends, loss in realizing their relationship was changing so quickly, and anger because her daughter did not consider Jane's feelings.

As discussed earlier, anger and related emotions may well be part of the Shift. Anger can be an unconscious way parents push their children away, and on their end, children might push their parents away by unconsciously doing things that provoke them, such as running off to a party instead of packing with mom.

The expectations that tainted the daughter's departure surfaced again when Thanksgiving vacation arrived. Jane couldn't wait to have some of the status quo back—to go shopping together, to have her daughter help with dinner preparations, and to share a little of what they called "stupid television" before going to bed. Instead, she got another surprise. Her daughter didn't show interest in doing any of those things.

> Her first visit home at Thanksgiving turned into a huge disappointment. What she wanted to do was call all her friends and go out with her high school friends—which she did. Then she would sleep late the next day, not even having breakfast or lunch with us. During her entire Thanksgiving vacation, she spent almost no time with the family. I felt angry the whole five days.

In this case, some of Jane's anger was self-directed. She realized she had never discussed her thoughts of what would happen when her daughter returned home from college. Her daughter continued to act as though she were still in college rather than part of a family. Some of Jane's anger was also rooted in disappointment. She thought that having her daughter come home for this first visit since she had left home would be like "getting her baby back." Instead, she got someone very different—a young adult who had developed a sense of autonomy.

Most parents want their children to grow into independence, but the desire does not come without ambivalence. The internal push-pull—wanting to move the child out the door while simultaneously wanting to pull her back into the nest—can sometimes be expressed as anger.

In a discussion of what most surprises mothers who have recently launched their children, life coach Tammy Hottenspiller puts the spotlight on anger:

It's not anger in the traditional sense in that it pertains to hostility. It's more of an anger that is wrapped up in disappointment, hurt, and frustration. This "anger" is three-fold: anger towards oneself for not preparing for life post raising kids; situational-anger that some children leave the nest and rarely look back; and anger towards the husband because he doesn't understand what she's going through.[6]

The prospect of facing unknowns can often trigger anger. The anger may sometimes mask fear because people don't know what to expect next. Author and counselor Greg Baker published an article entitled "The Relationship between Fear and Anger." In it, he describes the close relationship between the two, concluding that fear can often create anger.[7] For parents with an abundant, decades-long investment of emotional and intellectual resources in their children, life without them may be the biggest unknown they have ever faced. Fear, and the associated anger, can be perfectly understandable and typical responses.

Fear

Cathy says the most poignant aspect of the separation from her daughters, ages eighteen and twenty, is that they are "cognizant of my apprehension about being alone and want to help." They both invited her to visit any time, even though both are more than five hours away at their respective colleges. As a single parent, Cathy found herself wondering simple things like, "How much food should I buy? I don't even know how much food to buy for one person."

This did not signal a life-threatening fear; however, the prospect of being alone at home did cause her to feel distraught. "When my younger left home I had to close her bedroom door. Every time I walked by, I felt like my heart was going to jump right into my throat." She also referred to the "shock of being alone."

A "fear of fear" may be one reason why a parent would temporarily become a hummingbird, for example. She wants to avoid the
situation that she believes will trigger fear. In a *Psychology Today*
article about coping with fear, psychotherapist Linda Walter described the emotional vortex that some people experience:

> A major aspect of anxiety is the tendency to develop a *fear of
> fear*. In other words, becoming afraid when having feelings
> which we attribute to anxiety or fear, no matter what the rea-
> son. In this case, not only do we try to avoid the fearful situa-
> tion that has started these feelings in the first place, but
> the *feeling* of fear also becomes something we want to try to
> avoid. [8]

Fear responses are somewhat like a child standing on a diving
board, getting ready to jump for the first time. The fear may intensify before it subsides, and how long it takes to disappear completely depends on the individual. There is no predictable timeline, but once they dive in the water they can look back on their
accomplishment and quell the fear of diving the next time.

Excitement

The following excerpt is part of a story posted at the end of August
2012 by Jeanne Rollins, a therapist who maintains an online chat
site about parenting and families:

> When our youngest headed out, instead of waiting for the fog
> to lift I looked for peaks and discovered silver linings. I set out
> answering a question that simmered beneath the demands of
> our growing family: "What do I want to be when my kids grow
> up?" After happily forwarding the lives and dreams of others I
> was ready to get back to my own. I thought about how to make
> the best use of my new-found time. I embarked on a process of
> self-discovery much like we encouraged in our kids. I took a
> good look at my personality, skill set, interests and life experi-
> ence. [9]

Emily told me that throughout the twenty-three years she focused on her children, she tried to stay current in her field of physical therapy by reading. Unfortunately, competence in the new techniques and technology required hands-on experience. "I had to figure out my narrative," she said, "Why did I leave? What would I bring to the field in coming back?" Within a month of her youngest son's leaving home, she volunteered to assist at a regional rehabilitation hospital, hoping that she could gain the skills needed to return to her profession. Her first day, she was frightened, but absolutely thrilled at the prospect of being able to help people again. Within a few months, the volunteer position turned into a full-time, paid position that put her career back on track. She thrived in the environment, being back among colleagues again. Her participation in the workforce was a springboard toward development in both social and professional areas of her life.

Emily's phrase "figure out my narrative" struck me as very useful concept for anyone going through the Shift, particularly in trying to understand one's responses to it without being self-judging.

All of the responses described above are brief examples of people's journeys that involve emotions. It's important to focus on this because a number of articles and online postings about the experience of launching young adults seem to suggest that one can *decide* to get over "empty nest syndrome." In other words, they position the launch and resolution stages of the Shift as part of a largely cognitive process when, in fact, they are part of an emotional journey. For example, one article called "Coping with Empty Nest Syndrome" offers the following guidance on moving past any feelings of sadness or anxiety in a formulaic manner:

> You've spent some 18 years dedicating your life to caring for your children, and now that they've moved on to a new chapter in life, it's time for you to give yourself some much-deserved attention. Now's a great time to book that romantic getaway you and your spouse have been eyeing for years. You can also

finally tackle the projects that were simply not doable with a full house, like adding an addition to the home, remodeling the kitchen or setting up that home gym you always wanted.[10]

These ideas have merit, but moving past strong emotions is not like turning on or off a light switch. Keep in mind that while taking a vacation or remodeling a room in the house may quiet the intensity of the feelings, they can also be ways of bypassing the reality of your emotions. There is no formula or antidote to eradicate the feelings of anxiety, depression, anger, or fear that you might experience post-launch. Doing things to "give yourself some much-deserved attention" will not, in themselves, transform your emotional response to having your children out of the home.

It's important to recognize your feelings first, and then figure out ways to invest the free time you now have. When it comes to the emotional journey that is the Shift, there is no way around it but through it!

REFRAMING THE SHIFT

Reframing means to look at, present, or think of beliefs, ideas, or relationships in a new or different way.[11]

Different people might identify with parts or all of these stories. Feelings are fluid and may change from anxiety to sadness to anger, for example. This can be a difficult experience that can be mitigated when a person tries to look at her new and unfamiliar situation through a different lens. This reframing process can be very helpful in seeing opportunities instead of loss.

For example, many parents, particularly mothers, make every effort to be there when the children come home from school. After the youngest leaves, when the afterschool hour rolls around, the 3 o'clock blues may hit. The parent senses holes in their daily routine, and those empty spots in their schedule remind them that their children are gone. Their initial perception of the gaps might be a sense of loss and a sadness that the day seems so much longer than when the children were home. Reframing that experience could involve exploring the things that can be done with that additional time—taking a walk with a friend, scheduling an afternoon appointment with the dentist, volunteering at the library. Through the process of looking at the situation from a different perspective, gaps turn into portals, transforming something difficult, negative, and challenging into a picture of what's possible and positive.

That doesn't instantly take away the ache of the 3 o'clock blues. However, as days go on and a person gets in a different rhythm, 3 o'clock becomes less important. Soon, the parent looks at her watch and it's already 4 o'clock. This is an illustration of her Shift and the evolution through it.

Meredith Vieira offers two wonderful examples of reframing that she experienced after she had just launched her youngest. The first is a story of turning a time of transition, and potentially a feeling of loss, into a time of discovery:

> I felt so blessed that I was able to have three children. The notion of their leaving was bittersweet, even though I knew intellectually that was a good thing—that we'd done our job as parents. Right after I left the *Today* show [in 2011], my husband and I went to Cape Cod because I wanted to decompress. We went by ourselves. We hadn't done anything like that in all these years of parenting . . . we had a great time. I thought I would feel guilty about not encouraging the children to visit, but then I thought, "We have this great opportunity to create a fresh start for us." How wonderful to be able to do that.[12]

And then in 2013, after NBC invited her to come back to television and do a talk show, she decided to say "yes" to an opportunity that she found a bit disquieting. Her youngest was now through a couple of years of college and, with the encouragement of her husband and children, she decided it might be time to go beyond her comfort zone.

> When I left the *Today* show, I could not have imagined doing a daytime show . . . But you may be looking down the road and it

isn't the road you imagined. It might have curves and bends
that you wouldn't believe!

The fact that the children had launched allowed me to re-
launch. [13]

Reframing can be experienced as a way of stretching oneself—
doing something that is new and challenging. Meredith's show can
be seen as a new beginning, like becoming a new parent all over
again. Similarly, it is no coincidence that I started writing this book
when I did, just as my youngest was preparing to leave for college.
The desire to add another dimension to my life through the crea-
tion of this book reflects a desire to reframe the Shift.

THE NEW STATUS QUO

As parents advance at their own pace to a point where the Shift
sheds light on opportunity, they will likely find they are doing day-
to-day things differently. Their schedule starts to fill with activities
unrelated to parenting. Parents might also find their involvement
in the young adult's life diminishing.

For example, it would not be uncommon for some parents to
be able to answer the following question about their first-semester
college freshman: "Do you know what classes he's taking?" or "Do
you know his class schedule?" These are familiar questions for
parents who are used to paying close attention to their children's
lives. The parents who have been involved in every step of their
child's academic and social careers have a natural tendency to
continue to do so. Perhaps by second semester of freshman year,
however, the need for details might begin to wane. Those parents
may find themselves letting go enough to wait for the young adult
to call and say, "I'm excited about this two-hour class on Tuesdays
and Thursdays in marine biology," or "I can't believe I don't have
classes on Friday so I can go to the gym and catch up on sleep."

Parents used to knowing every hour of their child's schedule would naturally have difficulty with a new status quo of not being sure what the young adult is doing with his time. For them, it's not a matter of "have to know" as much as that's how it's always been. As in the story I told earlier of the professor and her students taking the same seats in the lecture hall, this need of a parent signals a desire to repeat something that has provided a sense of comfort and security. As the momentum of the Shift continues, it will likely mean the parent will move to a different seat.

It may be a challenge for the child, as well. Some might be used to having their parents sculpting their careers (high school, summer activities, and so on), so they might not have developed their own skill set to know how to navigate post–high school life independently. On the other hand, it might be a relief to have some degree of autonomy.

When counseling parents who are going through the Shift, I sometimes use a metaphor to help them visualize moving to a new status quo. It provides a picture of how parents might strengthen their young adult's independence skills.

At some resorts, and even some public beaches, it's common for maintenance people to show up early in the morning and rake the beach. Walking the beach is worry-free because nothing dangerous is underfoot. It's tempting for parents to want to "rake the beach" for their children to make sure nothing hurts them. At the same time, when children become young adults, it's important for them to be aware of potential dangers, to watch out, and proceed on their own. We have to rein in that impulse to rake the beach, and instead, teach our young adults that there will be things that get in the way of an easy walk. It's wonderful to have a beach that looks perfect—like a picture on a postcard—but that doesn't represent the landscape in real life.

During my interview with Meredith Vieira, she referred to how able her children were to venture into the world and how proud she and her husband are of their initiative and sense of responsibility. Her feeling is a common one for someone who has enjoyed parenting and invested a great deal in the quality of parenting—and it's as though the young adults acknowledge that by making it clear through their grown-up behavior that they have reached a turning point. The parents no longer need to go to great lengths to protect their children from the realities of the world. It's a turning point that, using Meredith's term, allows a parent to "re-launch."

There is another dimension to the change that Meredith also addressed, as did so many other parents I interviewed for this book. The turning point signals an evolution in the way that parents and their young adults communicate. The subject matter of their conversations, and how they process what's being said, moves toward a more adult–adult interaction. For each person, there is a level of appreciation—and hopefully, enjoyment—that is new and fulfilling.

THOUGHTS TO CONSIDER

While powerful emotions can take hold during the Shift, the concept of "empty nest syndrome" is a fallacy. An important life event can trigger serious responses such as chronic depression; however, that does not mean that the life event itself should be inextricably linked to the word "syndrome." My emphasis on the concept of *evolving* nest is a deliberate way of focusing on natural changes occurring in your home without children and the opportunity to view your home as filled with new opportunities rather than as empty.

In this chapter, you had your first glimpse of the results of a national survey conducted for this book; they were expressions of how parents remembered they first felt after their youngest child departed. Combined with the results of my interviews, these responses were grouped into five categories: anxiety, depression, anger, fear, and excitement. You might feel any or all of these emotions at different points in the Shift. Which categories seem to fit your feelings?

"Anxiety" was the most common response noted, probably because a great many of us feel anxious when facing the unknown. The Shift involves a series of unknowns related to your young adult, you, and your spouse or partner, so anxiety could come into play a number of times. You can begin to address it by identifying the issues or factors at the root of your feeling, and then creating a plan of action to address them.

For example, concern over a child with acute asthma going off to college is perfectly understandable. Problem-solve with your young adult to try to mitigate the feeling. Talk about what action he or she would take if an asthma attack occurred. Determine what measures can be taken in advance, such as letting the school clinic know about the condition or establishing a relationship with a local physician.

There will be very little you can do about some problems, of course. If your son or daughter does not get along with a roommate, there isn't much you can do about that directly. Nonetheless, you and your young adult can try to mitigate the anxiety by talking about the problem. Again, identifying the exact source of your concern can help you handle it.

Depression is experienced on a continuum. It is not unusual to feel sense of loss and sadness when the youngest child leaves the nest; however, when it interferes with day-to-day living, then it's time to consult a therapist or other mental health professional. Eating excessively or not eating much at all, sleeping excessively or suffering from chronic insomnia—these are signs that the depression is disruptive to your life.

Mild, intermittent depression responds well to exercise, which stimulates the production of endorphins in your body. These are neurotransmitters that promote a sense of well-being. Music can boost the process, so exercising to music you enjoy is doubly helpful. In general, make yourself feel good by taking steps to ensure quality sleep and good nutrition. Positive is built on positive.

Anger can rear its head in variety of forms. It can show up as irritability, shortness with people around you, and even impatience with yourself. If this sounds like you, consider the likeli-

hood that it is a side effect of the natural and mandatory separation of your child from you. The anger occasioned by this separation is often reflected by nagging, being critical, and even avoidance. If you notice yourself exhibiting these kinds of behaviors, try
to step back and identify when you first started to feel the anger or
a sense of annoyance. That may be very hard to do because you
may have a sense that it has persisted for quite some time.

One technique that can help is composing a list of five things
that are bothering you. Rate each one from 1 to 10, with 10 being
the most extreme. Let's say that one item on the list is that your
son or daughter, who is just weeks away from leaving for college,
has a messy room. Did the condition of the room always bother
you? If it ranks as a 4 now, did it rank as a 1 when he or she was a
freshman in high school? The exercise can shed light on the fact
that your emotions are heightened because of the changes going
on. It can help you identify issues that are really important and to
prioritize them, whereas you can look at others and conclude, "I
don't really need to be bothered about that." Your very awareness
that some items on your list hold more significance than others
should help bring your anger or annoyance down a few notches.

As with any of the other responses, if you have fear, the first
step toward quelling it is identifying the source. Your fear about
whether your daughter will acclimate quickly in college may have
its roots in your own difficulty acclimating, for example. Attempt
to separate your own history from your daughter's current experience. Your young adult brings a skill set and judgment to her new
challenges that are different from yours.

Anticipate what causes your fears to surface; that is, know your
triggers. It may be fear of being alone or fear for the safety of your
child in a new environment. What would alleviate these fears for
you? Think about the strengths of your marriage and friendships.
Calling a friend you can talk to about how you dread having a
house with "no noise" could go a long way to allaying your fear.
Talk with your son or daughter about your safety concerns so they
know how you feel.

Actions like this will mitigate your fears, even if they don't eliminate them.

If any of these highly charged emotions continually interferes with your friendships, marriage, work, or ability to enjoy hobbies and other downtime, it is time to talk with a professional. If other people express concern for your well-being, that may be another indication that it's time for a "look under the hood." If the feelings come and go, however, and seem to correlate to specific triggers, then try some of the steps suggested to reframe the Shift so that you can consciously move toward a new status quo.

4

LOOKING INSIDE THE NEST

Change is the law of life. And those who look only to the past
or present are certain to miss the future.

—John F. Kennedy

The soundness of your marriage, or comfort in your single life,
may face tests when your young adult leaves.

In some marriages and single-parent families, the young adult
may have been both a source of friction and/or glue in the family.
In the context of a couple, was she the only source of common
dreams and goals for them? Alternatively, did the child cause her
parents to lose sight of the common dreams and goals that brought
them together in the first place? With the young adult out of the
nest, they have space to explore a different perspective on their
relationship. Perhaps they can peer into the kaleidoscope of their
marriage, rotate the tube, and watch as the tumbling objects
present various colored patterns.

The same kinds of issues and opportunities can apply to the
single parent, who now has the space to consider the various ways
her new single life could take shape.

THE TECTONIC PLATES OF MARRIAGE

The event of children leaving home can illuminate the stresses as well as the harmonious give-and-take in a marriage. Studies such as those shown in this book have shown that many couples experience a rejuvenation of their enjoyment of each other once the pressures of day-to-day parenting are diminished. Studies noted later in this chapter have also focused on the prevalence of divorce between couples in their fifties whose youngest child recently left the nest. Increases in longevity have contributed to revised thinking about how young fifty now seems—coffee mugs, T-shirts, and birthday cards now carry the message "50 is the new 30"—and some people in their fifties may feel that a marginal marriage is not a productive use of their many active years ahead.

Some couples see fireworks in their future as their youngest child packs her bags for college. Based on my interviews and surveys, however, that doesn't appear to be the norm. More likely, ambivalence, confusion, uncertainty, and fear are some of the initial feelings about their intimate relationships that precision parents experience as their youngest child leaves the nest. This vignette captures a common response:

> [Shelly] had poured her life into her kids; they had come first. Now, as the last child got ready to leave, she was scared, really scared. "I don't even feel like I know my husband. I haven't been alone with him since I was 26. Our whole life has revolved around the kids. Now what will we talk about at the dinner table? What will we do on weekends? I don't even know if I have energy left to put into this relationship. And, I don't know if I want to."[1]

This is an example of someone who questions how her marriage will take shape and the disorienting effect it can have.

THE REBIRTH OF MARRIAGE IN THE SHIFT

When their young adults leave, parents may find an opportunity for discovery and examination of their marriage that can trigger a renewed sense of intimacy and commitment. Their excitement about being a couple might be reawakened. They feel satisfied with their parenting and look forward to having their interpersonal relationship develop, allowing them to expand as individuals and as a couple. Their children still play a significant role in their life together, but so does the marriage. Their marriage may have taken a backseat for many years, but they've always stayed in the car. Now it's time to move the marriage to the front seat!

A 2008 study by a team of University of California–Berkeley psychologists suggests why an empty nest may have beneficial effects on the parents' marriage. It wasn't that the parents in the study had more time together; it was that the time they spent together was more satisfying. In other words, couples found advantages related to quality, not quantity, of their time together. According to the study published in the journal *Psychological Science,* underlying some of the gain in quality was the fact that many study participants—all of whom were women—felt that the presence of their children had distracted them from their original relationship. In summarizing their approach and findings, the research team emphasized that their study not only focused on whether marital satisfaction changed in mid-life, but why it changed. They concluded, very specifically, that the increased satisfaction with marriages "was linked to the transition to an empty nest."[2]

Some of the underlying reasons were highlighted in a 2009 article in *The New York Times*, in which the author cited numerous recent studies, including the research done by the Berkeley team:

> After the birth of a child, couples have only about one-third the time alone together as they had when they were childless, according to researchers from Ohio State.

The arrival of children also puts a disproportionate burden of household duties on women, a common source of marital conflict. After children, housework increases three times as much for women as for men, according to studies from the Center on Population, Gender and Social Equality at the University of Maryland.[3]

The research team's use of the terms "household duties" and "housework" doesn't begin to suggest the magnitude of household responsibilities that many women handle throughout their years of raising children. Those responsibilities are not limited to things such as vacuuming and preparing meals, but rather encompass coordinating family activities, logistics related to the children's academic and social life, and so much more. These are nearly unavoidable strains on marriage for most families.

The process of getting reacquainted may not be a dramatic romantic moment, although that's certainly possible. Two people merely being near one another having a relaxing dinner and talking about what they did that day can contribute to an evolving closeness. By taking time out for each other, they are refueling their affection for one another; the positive effect builds on itself and helps to strengthen their growth together. After the shared venture of raising children, they can jointly appreciate a sense of accomplishment. Parenting together is important common ground. Standing on that ground, the couple can start to build new layers into their relationship. Like geological strata, each layer tells a story of development and change.

When their children were still at home, Susan and Jim still made time to go to the gym two or three times a week, but never at the same time. They would joke about the irony of both liking the torso machine, which was developed by a golfer to help golfers improve their swing: Neither one of them played golf. Through the years, they had always said, "Maybe when the children are gone, we'll give it a try." For their first wedding anniversary after their youngest son left for college, Susan gave them six lessons together with a local golf pro. After a first lesson of trying hard to get it right and laughing at their mistakes, Susan said, "That was fun!" Jim agreed, and they scheduled the next lesson immediately. Their love of the game was linked in part to their enjoyment of how they approached it. When they played together, they never kept score. They reminded each other of tips they had learned in their lessons. They found the time together thoroughly relaxing.

As they played more often, they would sometimes accept invitations to be part of a foursome with another couple. They forged new friendships with people in their community.

With some of her newfound extra time, Susan stretched in another direction that had interested her for years. She had always wanted to travel, but had not gotten the chance. When her youngest was in his senior year of high school, she started taking courses to become a travel agent. She and Jim benefited from her new profession by traveling together more often, playing golf wherever they went.

When a couple like Susan and Jim embarks on activities together—going to the gym together instead of separately, learning to play golf, taking the occasional trip, sharing a movie—they are connecting without the distractions they had when children were present. Their focus on each other is enriched by the way they cultivate individual interests. Susan and Jim didn't replace day-to-day parenting with golf or any other activity; there is no replacement for parenting. They did find ways to fill the time with activities that built up the foundation of their relationship and allowed them to expand and fuel it further. They reawakened aspects of their marriage that had remained relatively dormant for many years.

The journey toward a closer relationship has no standard pace of progression. In one article that appeared in July 2013, a father had a rather tongue-in-cheek way of describing the slow move toward greater intimacy with his wife. Starting off by saying that they had not had an extended conversation in years, he said that he and his wife were having breakfast together after their youngest child left home. They talked for a while, but the subject wasn't about deep emotions or plans for the future. The conversation was about their breakfast and current events. He came to understand that "We are, after all, out of practice"[4] and in time and with patience, they would hopefully be in synch once again.

Couples evolve a new rhythm in their relationship after the children leave—some at a slow pace and some at a faster one. The pace that a couple has in bringing the relationship to the "front seat" can depend on a number of factors. Perhaps they have discussed "bucket list" ideas they have in common; that is, what things they haven't yet tried or places they have not yet visited that they really want to experience. Another factor could be how well they sustained common interests through the years. They may not have had a chance to play tennis or go out to dinner on a regular basis, but they would do it occasionally; they kept the embers burning until they had the time to restart the fire. In the situation described below—again capturing the husband's point of view— the couple very likely had plans for doing things together start to take shape even as their daughter was applying for college. They were a couple of Red Sox fans who enjoyed the streets and offerings of Boston:

> Empty nesting lived up to my excited expectations about it. We went to Fenway Park, the Red Sox won, and we didn't need to rush home to see our kids while they were still awake. Of course, had we done so, we would have simply found an empty house. Instead, we strolled leisurely along Newbury Street, stopped a bit and eventually headed home.[5]

For some precision parents, like Cindy and Phil, their commitment to each other after the launch matched their investment of time and energy in parenting. After parenting five children, they focused on their marriage with enthusiasm.

Cindy and Phil married after graduation from college and Cindy had only been working as a librarian for a year when they decided to begin their family. For a total of twenty-eight years, both of them meticulously scheduled their time so they could participate in their children's lives. Cindy volunteered at the school library so she could use her education, but had the added benefit of being available to her children during the day. After their youngest child left, they rediscovered the joys of being spontaneous; it made them feel like they were dating again, and in some ways, it was even more gratifying than their early years together.

THE RISE OF DIVORCE IN THE SHIFT

In their 2012 study "The Gray Divorce Revolution," sociologists Susan Brown and I-Fen Lin open the statement of their results with the following statistic: "The divorce rate among adults ages 50 and older doubled between 1990 and 2009. Roughly 1 in 4 divorces in 2009 occurred to persons ages 50 and older."[6] To some readers, this might seem inconsequential were it not for the fact that the divorce rate declined for the rest of the population during that same period.

Brown, who is co-director of the National Center for Family and Marriage Research at Bowling Green State University, says one underlying cause is a condition she calls "empty-shell marriages—marriages that are okay, but not particularly satisfying for the individuals involved."[7] The presence of children in the home creates a sense of satisfaction for many couples that evaporates when day-to-day parenting no longer occupies a central part of their lives. When the young adult leaves, the marriage seems to lack purpose; there is no focal point for interaction.

An American Association of Retired Persons (AARP) 2004 survey called "The Divorce Experience: A Study of Divorce at Mid-life and Beyond" concluded unequivocally that there is one main reason many mid-life divorces did not occur earlier: "Overwhelmingly, children were the glue."[8]

I see a number of related dynamics that may lead to divorce as well. In some cases, children have been a source of friction between the couple and that feeling of discord was part of the family status quo. It distracted the couple from their interpersonal relationship. When the source of friction is gone, they may realize that years have gone by without their focusing on the marriage or each other.

A variation of marital neglect can also occur with a couple who were well-coordinated in their parenting, having a seemingly frictionless relationship. They might get along for years yet never really pay attention to each other. And then they may arrive at the realization that they have grown apart significantly. As playwright Lillian Hellman famously observed, "People change and forget to tell each other."

Another scenario involves couples who repress their emotions, such as anger and/or loneliness. The children might have served as a distraction from their marital discord. With them no longer home, the couple may have the space and perspective to recognize it. They may have years of pent-up frustration with each other that finally surfaces and may evoke several questions: "Is this all we have left?" "Is this what I want?" "Is this marriage worth saving?" Keep in mind the opposite can occur, too, in terms of positive emotion; that discussion occurs in the paragraphs above.

It is important to note that divorce is not necessarily equivalent to failure. In some cases, the debris of marital difficulty can get in the way of the relationship with the children, and by doing so, prevent the parents from moving through the Shift. Or the children's presence may have fostered an unhealthy attachment between the troubled couple and their children; again, that would hold them back in terms of going through the Shift. In short, divorce can be a positive experience that is integral to advancing in the Shift. In a *New York Times* op-ed that appeared just after Al and Tipper Gore announced the end of their forty-year marriage, Deirdre Bair, author of *Calling It Quits: Late-Life Divorce and Starting Over*, stated:

> For my book, I interviewed 126 men and 184 women who divorced after being married 20 to 60-plus years. And what surprised me most was the courage they showed as they left

the supposed security of marriage. To them, divorce meant not failure and shame, but opportunity.

> Men and women I interviewed insisted they did not divorce foolishly or impulsively. Most of them mentioned "freedom." Another word I heard a lot was "control"; people wanted it for themselves for the rest of their lives. Women had grown tired of taking care of house, husband and grown children; men were tired of working to support wives who they felt did not appreciate them and children who did not respect them. Women and men alike wanted time to find out who they were. [9]

As an adjunct to this take on divorce, Betsey Stevenson, assistant professor of business and public policy at the Wharton School of the University of Pennsylvania, has looked at the lifespan issue as a prominent part of the discussion of post-fifties divorce. Stevenson, who focuses on marriage and divorce in her research, notes: "Some of those marriages that in previous generations would have ended in death now end in divorce." [10]

Social attitudes toward divorce also changed dramatically in the years that baby boomers began dating and then married. A comprehensive study in the *Journal of Marriage and Family* found documented an unrelenting trend in the final four decades of the twentieth century toward "increased acceptance of divorce, premarital sex, unmarried cohabitation, remaining single, and choosing to be childless." [11]

The question of why there is such a dramatic rise in divorce for this age group has multiple answers, but the AARP has some interesting insights as a result of its survey. While the survey did note that children had been the glue in many of the marriages that ended, it did not jump to the conclusion that merely having no children in the home prompted the divorce. The survey explored some personal motivations for moving toward a new life, not simply away from an old one. Citing the AARP's study, the *Wall Street Journal* noted that the upward trend in mid-life divorce "springs at least in part from [baby] boomers' status as the first generation to

enter into marriage with goals largely focused on self-fulfillment."[12]

AARP also found that 66 percent of the divorces in this age
group were initiated by women. The results of various studies and
surveys dovetail with this statistic in a very interesting way.

While doing research for his book *The Power of Risk*, author
Jim McCormick interviewed 189 female subjects about their inclination or aversion to nine different types of risk-taking: physical,
career, financial, social, intellectual, creative, relationship, emotional, and spiritual.[13] He found that women's risk inclination
spiked throughout their mid-forties through mid-sixties, which are
the primary years of what Gail Sheehy calls the Age of Mastery of
"second adulthood."[14] Sheehy notes:

> The stage after 45 is exciting more and more women to soar
> into the unknown. As family obligations fade away, many be-
> come motivated to stretch their independence, learn new
> skills, return to school, plunge into new careers, rediscover the
> creativity and adventurousness of their youths, and, at last, lis-
> ten to their own needs.[15]

The messages in the work of both McCormick and Sheehy, of
course, also apply to people who find new energy in their marriages.

It is important to note that neither extreme—divorce or a rich-
er appreciation for the marriage—is likely to occur overnight.
Changes in the marital life of parents going through the Shift can
take years as feelings, circumstances, and a new status quo at
home take shape.

RESHAPING A SINGLE LIFE

As noted in the opening of this book, parenting has evolved in the
course of just one generation. One of the most significant changes
is that single-parent households are now commonplace. In her

2012 book, *Don't Say I Do!* Orna Gadish notes the importance of society's destigmatizing single-motherhood in relation to the growing number of single-parent households: "Whereas women in the past faced very difficult and intense societal pressures for being [single parents] . . . today's women have been granted much more flexibility."[16]

Until the latter part of the twentieth century, many families stayed together at all costs. In addition, it was taboo for single women to bear children—the phrase "born out of wedlock" was said in hush tones and with scorn—and if they did, they met rebuke and/or pity for trying to raise them alone. In general, society's point of view has changed and one indicator is that a number of companies now provide childcare for employees; marital status is not a factor in their decision to provide such services.

Combining this societal change in attitude with the fact that people face circumstances that unintentionally thrust them into the role of single parent, it is easy to see why there is an increasing number of single-parent households.

According to the 2000 U.S. Census, an estimated 13.5 million single parents had custody of 21.7 million children younger than twenty-one years of age whose other parent lived elsewhere. And as of 2000, more than 1 in 4 families with children under the age of eighteen were headed by a single parent. In 1965, the number was 1 in 10. In addition, more than 3 of 4 single-parent families had a mother as head of household,[17] with single defined as divorced, separated, and never married.

Single parents have unique challenges related to raising their children. They may feel the need to put opportunities for companionship on the back burner, and divert more of their retirement money to a college fund than the couples they know. They may be stretched so thin in terms of time and resources that life after the young adults leave could represent an opportunity to breathe, to relax, and to enjoy their freedom. They may see the launch of their young adults as representing an even greater sense of the possibilities ahead than their married counterparts, allowing them to focus on themselves as individuals. Now that they have more free time, they may be more available for dates, a chance to advance their career by being able to travel more, dinners with friends, exploring hobbies—essentially exploring their own needs and hopes more than they could before.

On the other hand, a home with children may have represented such a safe and loving environment to them that the departure of the children might involve an acute sense of loneliness and vulnerability. Their life had an element of security and predictability in knowing that their center of attention was the children. Their evolving nest without children there on a daily basis might therefore be very unsettling. Putting the focus on themselves instead of children, and starting a new life without them, could be daunting. In this case, it is helpful for the single parent connect with other people, and pursuing involvement in career, hobbies, and/or volunteer activities becomes very important in moving through the Shift.

Debbie intended to be a mother regardless of her marital status. After two unsuccessful marriages, at the age of thirty-two she decided to become pregnant and become a single parent. She had a well-paying job in Silicon Valley and the confidence that she could afford the child without anyone's help. Throughout her child's early life, she took him shopping, to parties, and everywhere else she went. No babysitters for her little boy, and no father. As a teenager, when he began exercising more independence, she feared loneliness. Just after her son graduated from high school, she got married and moved out of the nest she had occupied with her son since he'd been born. Perhaps she sought a partner because of a fear of loneliness, or perhaps she was just more available to have a relationship. It's a multifaceted situation arising in the space created by no longer parenting twenty-four/seven. The aspect of her situation that is relevant to the Shift, however, is that the thought of "losing" her son appeared to arouse a kind of panic. We could say with logic, if not certainty, that Debbie sought to reshape her singleness by literally leaving it—and her newly emptied nest—behind.

When Kelsey's children left, she experienced a sense of relief that she no longer had to have regular contact with her former husband. She started to see things around the house that had not changed in years in her effort to maintain consistency for the children—photos, knickknacks, and even the arrangement of furniture. Following their departure, she got inspired to redecorate and rearrange. She no longer felt compelled to keep her former life front and center for the children's sake.

Julia, also a divorced and single mom, took a more drastic approach than Kelsey by removing all semblance of her old life. When her twin boys left home, she went to her manager and asked for a transfer to Germany, a country she felt at home in because she'd been born there in a U.S. military hospital. It was a dramatic leap into the resolution stage of the Shift—one that afforded her a modicum of familiarity and a great many unknowns.

Kelsey and Julia fall on opposite ends of the spectrum in terms of moving through the Shift and adapting to life after their children's departure. One evolved her nest and the other left it physically far behind. Debbie is somewhere in the middle.

Whether the changes are dramatic or simply tweaks to the nest, they can provide a sense of completeness, satisfaction, and optimism. This is true whether it is a couple making the changes together, or a single parent making them on her own. Refeathering the nest occurs at a different pace for different people—but it does eventually occur as the couple or the single parent experiences the growth and transitions that are integral to the Shift.

THOUGHTS TO CONSIDER

The shifts in the dynamics of a marital relationship can seem like the shifts in the tectonic plates composing the Earth's surface. In addition, the components of a marital relationship, like the Earth's tectonic plates, are always moving and adjusting in relation to each other. While the movement continues after the children leave, different dynamics come into play and the adjustments to them can take time. It is part of a gradual process during which a couple might rediscover the reasons they came together in the first place.

On the other hand, the departure of the youngest child might result in the couple realizing that the plates no longer seem to fit. They rub and hit uncomfortably. The couple can come to realize that the presence of their children contributed to a dynamic that allowed them to work together. Their focus on their children distracted them from focusing on stresses otherwise present in the marriage. Now that the children are gone, the stresses become more palpable.

The adjustments vary from couple to couple and depend on the substance, durability, and flexibility of the bonds of the marital dynamic. If you think you are experiencing signs of stresses in your marriage, it is important to be aware of them while articulating and evaluating them. Consider the uniqueness of your marriage with an open mind and how it may not fit someone else's definition of "good" or "great," or even survivable.

Warning signs include leading parallel lives. You inhabit the same house and have a sense of business-as-usual, but your paths don't intersect in any meaningful way. Another warning sign is a lack of enjoyment when you do spend time together. Another is a constant sense of being misunderstood or not being heard.

These signs do not automatically result in irreparable or cataclysmic stresses in your marriage. However, if you are concerned by discovering warning signs in your marriage, then consultation with a marital therapist is a prudent next step. Professional marital therapists take many forms. They can include licensed marital therapists, clergy, psychiatrists, and others trained specifically to help couples understand and address the stresses in their marriage.

Single parents could have a broad range of situations, depending on how long and under what circumstances they became single parents. After being solely responsible for raising one or more children, the departure of the youngest could mean liberation or loneliness, or a mixture of both.

Single parents in a committed or developing relationship have additional capacity to focus on companionship with someone other than their child. Single parents who are not in such a relationship might feel more of a sense of loss or loneliness because their primary companions, perhaps for many years, have been their children. It is understandable that they might even feel despair. Strengthening and developing other relationships is vital and there are many direct paths to doing that.

Single parents outside of a committed relationship also have the opportunity to apply their additional capacity to develop existing or new interests. For example, one of your gifts may be singing. Joining a choral group helps you express a talent and make friends. If you have wanted to do community service and never had the time, perhaps you have it now.

The rebirth of a marriage, questioning the viability of a marriage, and the reshaping of a single life capture three different Shift experiences. With a couple, fulfillment and satisfaction can be realized over a short or long period of time and with or without professional help, depending on the marital dynamics. The optimism and growth in a single parent is realized the same way. Regardless of your status, whether your marriage is strengthened or dissolved, or whether you are a single parent, there is always the opportunity for fulfillment and satisfaction.

5

REMINISCING ABOUT YOUR PARENTING

Trust yourself. You know more than you think you do.
——Dr. Benjamin Spock, *Baby and Child Care*

Assessing your parenting is a way of moving into a different stage of the Shift. The goal of reflecting on your parenting is to come to terms with where you are in this life phase so that it's possible to keep moving toward resolution.

As parents, it is natural to feel we could have improved upon things or done them differently; conversely, there may be things we're really proud of. There is a great deal of value in being able to identify and come to terms with parenting successes and regrets. Regardless of what we might have thought as we were reading all those parenting books while raising our children, there is no gold standard, no state of perfection, in parenting. Reconciling the successes and regrets helps us feel a sense of resolve; it helps in moving through the Shift.

LETTING THEM TAKE THE FALL

Some parents remain at the threshold of the Shift and may be stuck on autopilot. This may be seen when a parent continues to manage the child's life as they always have. Autopilot is a default way to proceed because of its familiarity to both the parent and child. The parents are involved in choices such as what college courses the young adult should take, what clubs to join, and what would make an acceptable major.

The Wall Street Journal has cited studies documenting that a trend is taking shape that reflects some young adults' desire to even involve their parents in their work life. The article states:

> Millennials—people born between 1981 and 2000s—are much closer to their parents than previous generations, and they have gained a reputation for being coddled by so-called helicopter parents, say researchers who study Millennials.[1]

The featured studies—one conducted by Adecco,[2] a company providing human resources services, and the other by PricewaterhouseseCoopers—focused on various ways that parents retained a firm foothold in their young adults' lives, including choice of job, participation in job interviews, review of job offer letters, assistance with securing promotions, and receiving copies of performance reviews.[3] Although the percentages of young adults who acknowledged that level of involvement were not high, the author of *The Wall Street Journal* article incorporated various sources supporting the assertion that involvement of parents in a young adult's career is a growing trend.

Parents who are tempted to jump into their young adult's work life might keep a famous Mark Twain quote in mind: "A man who carries a cat by the tail learns something he can learn in no other way." Once there is momentum toward the resolution stage of the Shift for the parent and independence for the young adult, sustaining it has benefits for both.

There is a balance between being involved as an interested parent and micromanaging a young adult's college or other post–high school experience, or having a pronounced role in the post-college experience. If parents are unable to find that balance, they can remain in pre-Shift mode, essentially repeating the same kind of parenting they have always done. Continuing the same parenting style impacts both the relationship with the young adult and the parents themselves. It keeps them frozen in time and, instead of the relationship with the young adult evolving, it maintains a relationship that fosters the young adult's dependence on the parent. Dr. Madeline Levine, psychologist and author of *Teach Your Children Well: Parenting for Authentic Success*, focuses on how harmful this is to the child:

> The central task of growing up is to develop a sense of self that is autonomous, confident and generally in accord with reality. If you treat your walking toddler as if she can't walk, you diminish her confidence and distort reality. Ditto nightly "reviews" of homework, repetitive phone calls to "just check if you're O.K." and "editing" (read: writing) your child's college application essay.[4]

Despite the fact that they don't have the wisdom or experience of their parents, young adults need to be able to make choices independently. One of the ways they will develop wisdom and experience is through trial and error. *Amos 'n' Andy* was a radio show that ran in the United States from the 1920s through the 1950s and one of the popular exchanges of two of the main characters captures the challenge well:

> Kingfish: Well, good judgment comes from experience.
> Amos: Then where does experience come from?
> Kingfish: Experience comes from bad judgment.

Dr. Norman Rosenthal, a psychiatrist and author of the book *The Gift of Adversity*, brings the wisdom of this *Amos 'n' Andy* dialogue into the twenty-first century. Rosenthal wrote his collection of uplifting lessons and stories after losing his job at the National Institute of Mental Health. Parents going through the process of launching their children might find his insights relevant and useful. Particularly in thinking about letting young adults "take the fall," Rosenthal's thoughts on life challenges will likely resonate: "Mistakes are our best teachers, so don't waste them. Acknowledge them, learn from them, and become more competent because of them."[5]

It's not easy for parents to sit back and watch their young adult stumble. We have a knee-jerk reaction to try to soften or prevent the falls that result from bad judgment. It cannot be denied, however, that experience is the most effective teacher. Getting up from their mistakes and walking on their own is more empowering than anything parents can do.

WORKS IN PROGRESS

Many parents want a better or improved life for their children than the one they had growing up, regardless of their own childhood experiences. To try to create it, their degree of involvement in the child's life has notably increased from that of generations of parents in the twentieth century. It goes beyond knowing when the home games are and where next year's dance recital will be. Parents may go through gyrations to attend their children's events or to pick them up from school, even though a bus is available, to allow their children to attend extra-curricular activities. They want to provide them with as many opportunities as possible. Precision parents pay attention to every aspect of parenting: how to discipline, how to build self-esteem, and even how to develop a positive, loving relationship with their child.

In a parenting group I facilitate with young mothers, I heard one mother say that she never let her child watch television unless it was public broadcasting and only on weekends. Yet another mom said, "I let my children watch in moderation." A third mom chimed in, "I let my kids watch whatever they want." The discussion that followed these admissions illustrated something that happens frequently among parents. They compare their systems of checks and balances based on values, thinking, and a host of other factors. They look for signs in their children's behavior, and perhaps even affirmations from those around them, that their system is a good one.

Although it makes parenting sound a bit formulaic, the impetus behind these checks and balances is that parents think if they are moving in the right direction in a majority of the key areas, then their child will thrive. They seek knowledge about parenting both to *do* the best job they can and to have the comfort of knowing they really *tried* to do the best job possible.

It's easy to see how having a system of checks and balances would engender patterns of behavior and a predictable rhythm in the interaction between parent and child. That is appropriate until a certain age/stage. When the parent perpetuates that pattern as the child enters young adulthood, then the parent may be functioning on autopilot.

Two techniques that are often useful to parents who are stuck are learning to rephrase sentences and listening more. Rather than say, "I think you should . . . ," they ask a question: "What do you think about . . . ?" Asking more questions leads naturally to more listening. It is a way to cultivate independent thinking and move the child's perception of a parent from "mommy" to "mother." This is called a *parallel process*, because while the parents are teaching their young adult to think independently, they are helping themselves to let go and to move toward redefining their relationship so it's more balanced.

Another part of the process is parents asking themselves questions: "Does he need me to help with this?" "Is this a time when I should sit back and listen?" Questions like that will help parents feel less stuck in autopilot. Slowing down and thinking things through may not come as naturally as reverting to autopilot, at least at first, but they are essential measures to help parents move into the Shift. They reinforce the parents' ability to send the message to their young adult that she is no longer a child, but rather an accountable young adult. At the same time, the parent begins to realize: It's not that I am no longer needed—I'm just needed in a different way. Both are functioning on a continuum.

Writing for the *New York Times*, psychologist Susan Engel described the quandary caused by no longer knowing exactly how to parent young adults. Engel, the author of *Red Flags or Red Herrings: Predicting Who Your Child Will Become*, had just sent the youngest of her three sons to college:

> [When the children were young] you could fix many problems, and distract them from others. Your home could be a haven from all that might be painful and difficult in the world beyond. All of that changes when they are grown.[6]

Engel came to the realization that the parenting she had cultivated for decades was no longer relevant; it needed to evolve. Later in the article, she questioned her ability to parent young adults, since the requirements were so different from anything she had known before. She wondered if she was giving her sons the help they needed and wanted from her in coping with adult problems. In a conversation with one son, who was having a lot of difficulties with his graduate school program, he said something that helped her understand how she needed to evolve as a parent: "Mom, when I tell you what's wrong, I don't want you to tell me how to fix it, and I don't want you to tell me it's not as bad as I think. I just want your sympathy."[7] This is a good example of a young adult who is able to articulate what he needs. In this case, it was not answers he was looking for; he just wanted to be heard.

Another way of viewing the transition from parent of a child to parent of a young adult is that one's listening evolves. We take more time to hear what the young adult believes he needs rather than tell him what he needs from us.

COMMUNICATION

Advances in technology have added dimensions to the way we communicate with our children. The Pew Research Center issued a report about teenagers' modes of communication on March 19, 2012. It's a product of the Pew Internet and American Life Project, which issues reports on the impact of the Internet on families, communities, work and home, daily life, education, health care, and civic and political life. The Pew report affirms what most parents already know through experience: The number of texts per day is on the rise, older girls are the most enthusiastic texters—averaging about 100 texts a day in 2011—and most teens use texts about twice as often as they make phone calls.[8]

The instant, efficient communication we have with our children and young adults in the form of a short text means we can communicate with them frequently without it seeming like an intrusion on their time or ours. A text from mom asking "How did it go?" after her son's finals ended might get a texted reply of "K," or the son might call and provide some details. We hopefully take our cues from the young adult's response, to watch for the signs that he's ready for longer communication than a short text.

It's a remarkable contrast with the experience baby boomers' had communicating with their parents. For many who went to college, they faced the obligatory Sunday call—a collect call—to the parents to tell them what happened that week and what was planned for the coming week. There was no spontaneity, no ability to share something on a quick, casual basis.

In a way, then, we might want to look at mobile tools as a great gift to parenting. They enable us to keep in touch with our young adults and vice versa. According to the surveys I conducted, nearly half of the respondents indicated that they initiate contact daily with their young adult who left home within the past year by phone, email, text, Facebook, or some similar means. Roughly the same percentage indicated that their young adult initiates contact daily.

In response to the question "How often do you initiate contact with your young adult by text, email, Facebook, or phone?" survey participants indicated the following:

Daily	42%
2+ times/week	31%
Weekly	18%
Biweekly	6%
Monthly	3%

In response to the question "How often does your young adult initiate contact with you by text, email, Facebook, or phone?" survey participants said:

Daily	40%
2+ times/week	27%
Weekly	19%
Biweekly	7%
Monthly	7%

In high school, contact between a parent and child is probably daily, and many times a day, but may consist of texts from the child such as "Pick up at 4" or "at Jon's til 5." With the young adult in college, the communication might be a call about a class or activity. And as parents step back from the style of communication they had with their high school child, the communications will tend to be less directive. Rather than texting messages like "Be home by 6," the daily communication with the college-age young adult might just be a photo of a tree that fell on the neighbor's driveway.

One of the parents responding to the survey remarked, "We text each other all day long, but that will taper off as the years pass." Another respondent with four young adults out of the home indicated that the communication depended on the child: "Two call daily, one rarely calls, and the other calls several times a week."

Frequency of communication is not a clear determinant of how much a parent and young adult are evolving to an adult-to-adult relationship. It is the degree of mindfulness about the ways each communicates that signals how the relationship is maturing.

Spontaneous efforts to maintain connectedness can occur through many means, and the options keep increasing. Probably the most popular is texting. In my interview with Debbi O'Shea, the beauty blogger, she described texting with her son in college as "sound bites . . . texts are comforting to me. We've always been close and this is part of it. Just a couple of words back and forth mean a lot."

REFLECTION—A NATURAL PROCESS

Each person's life contains a variety of punctuation. Some moments suggest a pause in the flow, like a comma, whereas others signal a full stop, like a period. For some parents, taking their young adult to college as a freshman is the latter type. For them, it's a defining moment when day-to-day hands-on parenting stops; the natural thing to do next is start a new sentence in their story.

When writing, people will often go back and reread what's already been written so they can make sure they are satisfied with it. The author cannot help but wonder, "Did I say what I meant to say?" "Could I have said it better?" Reflecting on one's strengths and limitations as a parent is natural.

One of the survey questions I posed to parents whose children had recently left home was the following: "Currently, how would you evaluate your parenting?"

a. Overall I feel good about my parenting, but know that I wasn't perfect
b. I don't feel bad, but wish I could have done better
c. There's so much more I wish I would have known
d. I met the challenges as best I could
e. I have many regrets

Eighty-five percent of the respondents checked "a." The rest checked "b." Of note is that all of the parents described themselves as somewhere between "involved" and "extremely involved" in their child's life.

In discussions with parents, a common theme is that they appraise their performance as parents on the basis of criteria that relate to their young adult's success. They tend to focus on areas of their child's experience such as the following:

- Academic achievement
- Social adjustment
- Career choice
- Sense of values
- General happiness

For example, a couple who both have careers in law might have hoped their child would, in some way, follow their footsteps. At the same time, they want her to follow her own vision, and hope they have given her the space to do so. When they start reflecting on their parenting by considering their daughter's career choice, they might feel a twinge of disappointment that she chose something other than law. Perhaps both parents came from several generations of lawyers and saw the "family" talent for debate and analysis in their daughter. As she grew up and excelled academically, they would occasionally remark, "She would make a brilliant lawyer!" They found her decision to pursue a career in medicine laudable and had confidence that she would make a wonderful physician, even though they secretly hoped she could be outstanding in the field if she pursued law. Ultimately, when they considered other factors, any sense of disappointment dissipated when they realized she was thriving. Reminiscing about their parenting helped them see that, in terms of happiness, overall adjustment, and goals, their daughter was a young adult of whom they could be very proud.

In reflecting on their parenting, it's not uncommon for parents to be hard on themselves occasionally—to focus momentarily on

"I could have done better," rather than pat themselves on the back. A May 2013 survey by a *New York Times* reporter indicated that, for the most part, young adults are giving their parents kudos for trying rather than criticizing them for being overbearing or out of touch with them. Katherine Schulten posed a set of questions to teenaged and young adult readers that asked them to describe their parents' behaviors in relation to so-called helicopter parents. She asked them:

> How involved are your parents in your life? How much do they step in to help you with your schoolwork, social life, college applications, hobbies, sports or anything else? How often do they try to solve your problems? Do you like having their help, or do you find it burdensome? Why?[9]

Sixty-two comments quickly came in to the *New York Times* website. Some of them were quite detailed in answering each of the questions posed, and one respondent after another said unequivocally that their parents were not helicopter parents. What they described were what I have been referring to in this book as precision parents; that is, deliberate and diligent in their parenting, but not overwhelming. Comments like this were common: "My parents haven't stepped in recently because I haven't given them a reason to." The young respondents themselves also chimed in about what they thought was good parenting—and gave their parents credit for achieving it: "I think the perfect amount of help from a parent is enough to steer you in the right direction and to your full potential, but not enough that they do all the work for us."[10]

Part of the task of the Shift is to reconcile your own success and regrets in the parenting of your young adult. More importantly, part of the task is to recognize that your young adults are developing their own blueprints for their life, and they may be different from yours, or from what you'd hoped for. Additionally, they may not be compatible with yours.

Cheryl was a single mom who completed her Ph.D. degree in organic chemistry just before giving birth to her son, Sam. Sam grew up around chemists and, through the years, sat in on many of his mother's conversations with her research colleagues at the university hospital. He was absorbed into a community of people who enjoyed their work and were extremely diligent parents; they were a support group for Cheryl that made her life as a single mother much easier.

Sam decided to major in chemistry. The summer after his freshman year of college, he took a job in a breeding kennel and, suddenly, he decided he wanted to breed and train purebred dogs for a living. He told his mother he wanted to drop out of college and pursue his new passion.

Cheryl and her son agreed that it was important for him to return to college and complete another year of his studies. Cheryl told him if he still felt as passionate about working with dogs after that, she would do what she could to help him pursue that profession. During his sophomore year, Sam discovered that he really liked studying chemistry and he concluded he could combine his enjoyment of it with his love of animals by becoming a veterinarian.

This vignette captures a wonderful result of allowing a young adult to feel his way. College is a period of discovery and self-discovery. By taking a step back, Cheryl enabled Sam to explore his interests and his options, as well as figure out what kinds of things were really important to him in spite of her own hopes and desires.

Cheryl's reining in her opinion about what her son should study and how he should live his life is a very hard thing for many, if not most, parents to do. Precision parents may have an especially difficult time in allowing this process to take place because they are so used to playing a key role in shaping their children's pursuits—sports, academics, habits, and social life. They have spent years behind the scenes providing opportunities for their children. It may take an ongoing conscious effort for precision parents to remind themselves that the period after they leave home is supposed to be a time of exploration and discovery for their young adult. "Ongoing" is an important part of the message because it could take all four or five years of college, or even longer, for that young adult to figure out what career he or she wants to pursue. It's like creating a sculpture: You've envisioned what the outcome will be, but there are often surprises throughout the creative process.

Cheryl encouraged her son to explore and come to his own decision through his own experience; she knew her son and trusted his judgment. The understanding the two of them came to about his sophomore year helped her son come to his own decision about what he wanted to pursue on his own, to sift through different options to determine what felt right. In this way, Sam was able to facilitate his own independence.

During my interview with Nicki, she brought up an important reflection related to the tack that Cheryl took. It was about the value of listening more to her child when he became a young adult:

> It's taken me all these years to realize that providing a knee-jerk opinion if one of my children tells me something is not necessarily the best approach. I've learned the value of listening, of waiting for one of my children to ask me for my opinion. It was important growth for both of us.

Nicki's comment reminded me of a quote from the Greek philosopher Epictetus that applies in parenting, and in any relationship: "We have two ears and one mouth so that we can listen twice as much as we speak." It's a goal that we as parents may strive to achieve, but it's not easy to do!

THOUGHTS TO CONSIDER

Throughout the early years of parenting, it's customary to take a directive approach. The safety and well-being of a child depends on clear instructions from a parent. As the child grows into young adulthood, parents hopefully make the transition to offering suggestions on behavior or being Socratic and asking questions instead of providing answers. Just as your child's developmental changes occur over time, so do yours. It is important to become mindful of the need to evolve your parenting style and try to make adjustments.

Stepping back and allowing our young adults to make mistakes and grow from them is the most important gift we can give them as they mature. Otherwise, we deprive them of their ability to learn from their missteps and take responsibility for the consequences of their decisions. Challenging as it can be, we have to cultivate the ability to let them take the fall. By making mistakes, working through them, and recovering from them, young adults develop confidence in themselves.

Communication is a central element of change in your interaction with your child when he or she becomes a young adult. In many cases, it is often helpful to take the lead from your young adult, particularly after your son or daughter has departed the nest. While you can provide reassurance that you will be available to help, to a great extent, you also want to allow your young adult to initiate the pace and frequency of communication. It helps you as the parent and the young adult to redefine your relationship. That does not mean you cannot call occasionally or when you have concerns.

As part of the process you go through in modifying the timing of your exchanges, you will undoubtedly find yourself also making a conscious effort to change the content of your messages. Parents may have to fight the urge to text questions like, "Are you prepared for that exam tomorrow?" and "Have you done your laundry?"

Techniques that I find valuable in making thoughtful adjustments in one's parenting style can be summed up in these words: *listen, provide space*, and *less is more.*

Listen to how they talk about their challenges. As you do, think back to your own struggles and what you learned from the mistakes you made as you tried to handle them. Remember the bumps and bruises that taught you priceless lessons. Listening is an active parenting technique.

Give them space. Try to imagine your child playing with building blocks. He wants to make a castle and becomes frustrated when it doesn't look right to him. Your impulse is to want to help or do it for him, but what does he learn from that? In the end, it is trial and error that enables your child to build a castle. It will not look like the one you would have built; it will be all his. He will take pride in the result and gain from the experience.

Finally, consider how to make less into more. Put yourself on a word diet if you find yourself talking too much rather than listening. Step back and curtail your urge to help solve a problem; remind yourself of your young adult's strengths and ability to handle challenges. You can follow up by asking questions like "What do you think?," which hopefully will enable your young adult to slow down and think things through.

After all is said and done, there will always be areas that, as parents, we could have improved upon. Take strength in your love, hard work, and best intentions.

In reflecting on your parenting, use a wide lens. Take in the whole landscape of your parenting. You are a work in progress, just like your children. Many elements of the landscape have changed over the years, and they will continue to do so.

It is also a distinctive landscape. Each child comes with a unique set of personality traits, skill sets, and strengths. Each of us has to learn to parent according to that uniqueness. No book has been written with all the answers on parenting your child. By its nature, parenting involves trial and error.

Changes do not stop as you enter the resolution stage of the Shift, either. Your parenting will continue to evolve as your young adult matures. New challenges and opportunities await you as the child you raised marries, has a first child, and moves through the milestones and phases of life. Every one of them represents shifts in the relationship you have with your son or daughter.

We are all works in progress! Our development is like riding a bicycle: If we stop peddling, we don't go anywhere. Each of us needs to peddle at our own pace and appreciate our ability to keep moving forward.

6

CHALLENGES, UNCERTAINTIES, FEAR

I wanted a perfect ending. Now I've learned, the hard way, that some poems don't rhyme, and some stories don't have a clear beginning, middle, and end. Life is about not knowing, having to change, taking the moment and making the best of it, without knowing what's going to happen next. Delicious Ambiguity.
—Gilda Radner

Kelly was planning a very large family reunion in Maine. She visited the property where the cabins in which they would be staying were located in advance of the gathering. Not having been there in a number of years, she was surprised to see that the grounds had dozens of new buildings and roads, many of which had no street signs yet. She tried to use her GPS to guide her out of the maze, but it just directed her in a circuitous path. Since Kelly had thought she knew her way around the thousand-acre property, she hadn't thought about downloading the new maps for her GPS prior to her trip. It had no record of the new roads; she was lost.

This is how many parents I've spoken with and counseled began their journey through the Shift: It's as though their GPS for navigating the phases of life doesn't have updated maps. The experience may make them feel frustrated and perhaps even anxious as they face new territory. They may have a sense of confusion that feels pervasive. Their attempts to move ahead seem reasonable; however, they know they don't have a clear sense of their route.

RECOGNIZING SIGNS OF THE SHIFT

The early signs of the Shift do not tend to be obvious, especially when a young adult's development toward independence progresses in a conventional way. Life moves forward as the young adult gets a driver's license, applies for college, gets a part-time job, and so on.

In some cases, however, the young adult does not progress in a typical way. Parents in this position may experience a sense of anxiety when their young adult's pace of development is out of synch with his or her peers. They may have difficulties coming to terms with the delays in the launch. It is important not to view this as a failure of parenting; the rate of development toward autonomy is, to some extent, an individual matter. The launch will happen, though, and once they accept the fact that their young adult is simply developing at his or her unique pace, they can move on.

A look at both situations provides different perspectives on the challenges, uncertainties, and fears associated with the Shift.

When Young Adults Are in Launch Mode

Perhaps you were immersed in parenthood for most of your adult life, paying attention to every detail of your children's life. Of course you noticed changes in their bodies and demeanor; however, those changes occurred over time. And you adjusted over time, watching them learn to walk on their own, then teaching them to ride a bike, letting them go to sleepovers, and so on. Throughout those changes, they always lived at home.

Their presence was the one constant in a fluid situation; it helped create a status quo. Both parent and child had a consistent reassurance that the other was nearby. Although the parents were letting go as the child moved into young adulthood, that process was almost imperceptible much of the time. Certainly, there were rites of passage like learning to drive and getting a part-time job that served as reminders of change; however, the parents were involved in those exercises in autonomy. All of these developmental markers occurred within the confines of the nest; it was the safe haven for trial and error.

On a cognitive level, you knew intellectually your children would leave someday to build an independent life. On an emotional level, though, you had no reliable way to predict how you would feel. You had no map for that next part of your journey as a parent—no clear sense of roads or landmarks ahead. However, if you know where you are, you improve your chances of figuring out where you're going. With that in mind, your awareness of the signs of the Shift and your responses to it will hopefully help you begin to "update your maps."

It is no coincidence that I started writing this book a year before my youngest left for college. I recorded my thoughts and feelings at moments along the way to give myself insights into my own experience of the Shift. That awareness gave me some clarity about how to conceptualize the Shift.

Liz and John have two daughters who are close in age. The older daughter chose to attend a college close to home and to live at home, so life with her didn't change all that much when she became a freshman. That same year, the sixteen-year-old daughter got a part-time job at a clothes store. Her parents encouraged her, knowing that she'd had an interest in fashion and thinking she could learn about responsibility and handling money while doing something she enjoyed. They also thought her sales job at the store might help her refine her career choice. One day, they saw her W-2 form on the kitchen table. Their "little girl" was making money and paying taxes. When the parents saw that tax form, they realized their daughter was demonstrating signs of maturity and having important exposure to an adult world. It signaled the fact that, in the not too distant future, she would be leaving home.

Signs of the Shift can be external, sometimes symbolized by tangibles like the daughter's W-2, or they can be internal—a felt sense of change.

Disruption of family routines is a common example of an external sign. Routines such as Sunday dinner provide a sense of stability and comfort. It's a pattern established usually early on in family life as a way of connecting. As part of the Shift, the predictability associated with routines like this starts to dissolve. You prepare a Sunday dinner as usual, but your daughter calls and says that she'd like to stay at her friend's house for the evening. Other elements of the routine begin to disappear, too, as your child makes choices that reflect the desire to be with peers and apart from family.

The internal signs are thoughts and emotions that contribute to a sense of disorientation. One moment, you have a sense of longing for the time when your children needed to hold your hand to walk. Moments later, you find yourself cheering them on inside because you see them making independent choices. In all likelihood, your feelings vacillate; emotionally, it might feel as though you're standing on sand moving beneath you, causing you to lose your footing occasionally. Feeling unsteady in the Shift is normal.

Signs of the Shift can be seen in the changes in the nature of the relationships you have with your children now that they have entered young adulthood. As children, they needed a mommy and a daddy; as young adults they want a mother and a father. They evolved from being dependent on you for many day-to-day things to needing someone to bounce ideas off of and provide reassurance that their choices are sound. Hopefully you are able to have a Socratic dialogue, posing questions about values and decisions, rather than perhaps taking an authoritative approach as you might with a young child. That is, you give them more space to figure out who they are and what they have to contribute. This reflects how your parenting style changes as they mature. You may become aware of that change and reflect on the significance of it, not only in terms of your children's move into young adulthood, but also your own changes in behavior, communicating, and so on. This awareness could be an early sign of the Shift.

That said, some parents maintain the same style of parenting they have used throughout the time they were raising children, even after the young adults have left the nest. The manner of interacting and the nature of conversation do not perceptibly change. The college freshman may call and ask, "What classes should I take next semester?" or "What do you think of this sorority I'm thinking of pledging?" In a sense, then, the relationship is stuck in time. Parenting as though you are frozen in time may hinder the journey through the Shift as well as impede the young adult's climb toward independence.

Having recognized signs of the Shift, you may reflect on your current way of parenting: Has it changed? Has it remained the same? As the insights from psychologist Susan Engle suggested in the last chapter, the parenting you have spent decades shaping and refining is not the parenting you need when your child becomes a young adult. Parenting needs to evolve as the nest evolves.

When Young Adults Are Not in Launch Mode

Peter Spevak, a child psychologist and author of *Empowering Underachievers*, specializes in counseling children and young adults with social, academic, and/or maturational issues.[1] With few exceptions, the parents of these young people would fit my description of precision parents; that is, they are diligent, deliberate, and involved parents. Typically, these parents have always assumed that when their children became young adults, they would attend college immediately after high school. For the most part, however, Spevak's young adult clients were not ready for an independent life at the same pace as their peers. In his experience, they usually do move toward independence, but the path might be circuitous.

In the past couple of decades, American society has been expanding its view of the way children and young adults develop, with much more attention being given to the individual nature of growth. Many books address the reality that a so-called customary pace of progress really isn't so customary; for a number of young adults, the fact that they are not ready to move directly into college or a job after high school has no negative undercurrents. They likely have the same world of opportunities as their peers and will simply take a different path to discovering and exploring them. Numerous gap-year programs offer internships, academic enrichment, multicultural experiences, and much more to support the young adult in maturing and exploring at his own pace. In this way, North America is becoming more in step with Europe and Australia. Studentawards.com describes the advantages of the gap year in a way that illuminates why there are tremendous advantages for young adults who don't feel ready to go straight from high school to college:

> [A gap year] allows young people to regroup, to reflect and to experience life while learning more about themselves—the kind of thing you can't do in the classroom. It's only just starting to make an appearance in North America. That's why taking a year out is still seen as an unusual destination after high school or university, and feels like it's an innovative way to approach the next chapter in a young adult's life.

> The gap year has been around for decades in Europe and Australia where it's a household term. You're considered weird if you don't take a gap year. In the UK alone, each year approximately 230,000 people take a gap year. In fact employers in the UK are more interested in what you did in your gap year than what you did for an undergraduate degree. Generally the gap experience includes mixing academics, volunteer work and travel. It is supported by British Universities and colleges where students with gap year plans are regularly granted deferred admission—you don't have to reapply or negotiate individual deferment. . . . The gap year is regarded as a chance for students to develop skills and to take personal responsibility as an adult.[2]

There are myriad reasons why a young adult might not develop in a kind of "textbook fashion," but this is outside of the scope of this book. The very fact that the young adult does not seem to progress in the way the parents had hoped may alter the pace of the Shift. Parents have to adjust their thinking and reset their expectations to match the reality of their child's situation. They have to parent according to the child's needs—know your customer!—and allow the child to evolve toward a state of readiness at a pace that is appropriate for them. For those who aren't ready to separate from the nest, it would be useful for the parents and young adult to look around at the many gap-year programs. Having a launch occur on an individual schedule is a relatively common phenomenon and can even be considered an opportunity.

Mary Tuggle Payne describes her personal challenge in an article entitled "Not Quite Ready for College at 17." She begins with the statement, "In all of the planning we have done as parents for the future of our teenage daughter, we never thought we would be *Here*."[3] Payne's meaning of "here" is the point at which her seventeen-year-old daughter had not taken steps that got her any closer to college, or even to a driver's license. Payne describes herself and her husband as "achievers" who seem desperately eager to go through the launch.

Like Payne, there are many parents who recognize that a life phase is not taking shape for them the way it is for their friends. Their challenges, uncertainties, and fears are different from those of parents whose nest is evolving at a somewhat more conventional pace. While this may be difficult, it's important to keep in mind that the evolution is still occurring, even though the pace seems slow and varies from those around them.

RESPONDING TO SIGNS OF THE SHIFT

Preceding chapters introduced descriptions of how different people experience the Shift. As discussed earlier, one way to consider the responses is to draw a parallel with Elisabeth Kübler-Ross's five stages of grief—denial, anger, bargaining, depression (or sadness), and acceptance. While generally associated with the death of a loved one, these stages are widely recognized to have relevance in any situation involving a profound sense of loss. In a note to me about her post-launch feelings, author Janai Lowenstein conveyed her experience of the stages. She opened with some notes suggesting sadness and denial:

> "Empty" is a strong sensation that easily fills the mind and the pit of the stomach, as well as the heart, when it comes to a nest being vacated that once was bustling with activity. . . . It was a time for me that nothing else could "fill" that which was missing.

> I discovered I was attached so much to that part of life that I didn't want to let go. All my life was centered from childhood around the idea of having children. I hadn't spent any time longing for the time they would be gone. So I stayed attached to the dream of having them in my nest. I liked how I felt with them there.[4]

It is reasonable to envision that "staying attached to the dream" is also a strong impetus to engage in bargaining behavior. In fact, Janai's words capture beautifully how Elisabeth Kübler-Ross talks about conditions that give rise to bargaining behavior: The person feeling loss imagines there is a way to postpone, or even prevent, the inevitable.

At some point, Janai fully acknowledged that she was grieving. She felt "waves of hollowness through me, being sad, sometimes longing, sometimes loss." There was even a tinge of anger in remembering that the spaces in her life that had been filled with children were not anymore because "my children were now gone." As noted in chapter 3, this is not anger in the sense that it is grounded in hostility, but rather wrapped up in disappointment, hurt, and frustration.

Ultimately, however, Janai's feelings gave way to a sense of resolution; she felt satisfied that she'd done the best job she could.

Janai recognized that the need to care for her grown children "had to be transformed into a new kind of caring." She mentioned that it was a struggle to grasp her reality, but she had a sense of resolve in knowing that her children were well on the way to becoming mature adults.

Understanding the application of Elisabeth Kübler-Ross's work is a useful complement to the more archetypical approach I took with the hummingbird, eager beaver, and stunned deer. During those days or weeks when a person exhibits hummingbird behavior, she tries to evade the emotions that come with a sense of loss, as if moving quickly will enable her to stay a step ahead of them. When someone is in an eager beaver phase, activities focused on managing changes in the nest could be another way of sidestepping emotions. The eager beaver may intellectualize as a way of avoiding the full experience of feelings. If a person has the experience of feeling like a stunned deer, there is a paralyzing sense of being overwhelmed by emotions associated with loss. It is important to keep in mind that each of these responses can occur to varying degrees, and experiencing one might catapult the person into another phase.

In all likelihood, you related to some of the emotions and behaviors described above more than others; perhaps you even thought, "I remember feeling that way," or "I used to do that." In other cases, you may have concluded that you would "never" feel or behave in a particular way. Hopefully, in this chapter, you will start building on those concepts and begin to better understand how your feelings are changing within the evolving nest.

Identifying Where You Are Now

In surveying parents nationwide, I posed a number of questions to get a sense of respondents' parenting circumstances and to find out a few key facts about their experience of the Shift. As a way of beginning to explore your own experience of the Shift, consider how you would answer these questions that relate to interaction with your young adult and feelings about him or her leaving the nest to build an independent life:

How would you describe your parenting style?

    a. I am extremely involved in my child's life.
    b. I pay attention to my child's life and am involved quite a bit.
    c. I try to know what's going on in my child's life, but give him/her a lot of space.
    d. I wait for my child to involve me in his/her life.
    e. My child is very independent.

How would you describe the parenting style of your spouse or partner? (If you are a single parent, please indicate the parenting style of the person with the next greatest involvement in your child's life, such as a grandparent or other relative.)

    a. Extremely involved in your child's life.
    b. Pays attention to your child's life and is involved quite a bit.
    c. Tries to know what's going on in your child's life, but gives him/her a lot of space.
    d. Waits for your child to involve the person in his/her life.
    e. Your child is very independent.

How would you rate your level of emotional response to your child leaving home and establishing an independent life?

    a. It greatly upsets me; it signals an emptiness.
    b. It upsets me, but I realize this was inevitable.
    c. It upsets me a bit; I wanted to slow down the transition so it was not so abrupt.
    d. I'm delighted, even though I do miss him/her.
    e. I'm starting to enjoy the next stages of life.

My first feeling about my child leaving home was probably

    a. Anxiety
    b. Depression
    c. Anger
    d. Fear
    e. Excitement

When my child first left home, I sensed that my spouse/partner/other seemed mostly consumed by

    a. Anxiety
    b. Depression
    c. Anger
    d. Fear
    e. Excitement

How often do you initiate contact with your child by text, email, Facebook, or phone?

    a. Daily
    b. 2+ times/week
    c. Weekly
    d. Biweekly
    e. Monthly

How often does your child initiate contact with you by text, email, Facebook, or phone?

    a. Daily
    b. 2+ times/week
    c. Weekly
    d. Biweekly

   e. Monthly

How would you describe the way you're handling the extra time now that your child is gone?

   a. Bored
   b. Keeping busy in a random way
   c. Beginning to explore options
   d. Enjoying free time
   e. Using time differently

How would you evaluate your parenting?

   a. Overall I feel good about my parenting, but know that I wasn't perfect
   b. I don't feel bad, but wish I could have done better.
   c. There's so much more I wish I would have known.
   d. I met the challenges as best I could.
   e. I have many regrets.

Survey results indicated a direct correlation between parents' level of involvement in their children's life and their sense of loss and/or disequilibrium when the young adults left home. It is important to note that there is no judgment associated with that—no right or wrong, good or bad. As Janai expressed in her note to me, a heart-felt sense of "I really miss my child" can be inextricably linked to an understandable and common feeling after having immersed oneself in parenting for eighteen-plus years. In addition, Janai is among the many women I've spoken with who said they wanted to be a mother from the time they were young. Whether a woman shares that experience or decided later in life to become a mother, the feeling of disorientation when the children are gone would not necessarily be any different.

If your young adult is still at home, but preparing to leave in the not-too-distant future, then your perspective on the survey questions is anticipatory. You might feel very differently after your child actually departs your nest. A few months or a year from now, therefore, you will probably want to come back and review the questions to see how your answer might change when you have the perspective of someone who has gone through the launch. Your experience will evolve depending on where you are in the Shift.

Similarly, if your young adult recently left the nest, I encourage you to answer the questions in terms of what is true for you now, but come back to them in a year. Having had the time to see how your young adult is maturing and making adult choices may give you a fresher and even more positive perspective on your parenting skills.

Perhaps the survey questions can also stimulate some reflection on your changes in behavior—for example, how communication styles and habits with your children have changed. When you were in the anticipation stage and your child was still in high school, consider the frequency with which you called or texted each other and the topics you addressed. Both may have changed quite a bit when your child moved out of the home. When the children were in high school, communication may have happened periodically throughout the day and had a pragmatic purpose. Your exchanges may have been mostly about logistics in high school, for example—"What time shall I pick you up after basketball practice?" or "What time do you need to be at Brit's house?" After the young adult leaves home, there is probably a notable difference in the content and context of your exchanges. It's often no longer about practical issues as much as it is a matter of checking in and updating on what is going on in their lives. The young adults may share snippets of their daily life or just check in with their parents. Often parents respond in kind, taking their young adult's lead.

While I was writing this book, some of my friends mentioned that their young adults in college had already submitted applications for a semester abroad for the following year. My own sense of urgency had been triggered, as this was something our son had said on several occasions he wanted to do. I brought up the subject with my husband: "Our son hasn't mentioned anything about this! Should I call and remind him?" Referencing my own insights on communicating with young adults, he reminded me, "Wendy, navigating these issues can be as hard as seeing the dandruff on your own shoulder." Stepping back, we decided we would let the issue unfold in its natural course, allowing our son to take the initiative in planning. We would be there to help if he wanted our input.

Whether you are anticipating the launch, in the middle of it, or just past it, the exercise of going through the survey questions will likely help you in identifying emotional responses to the changes occurring in your life and your nest. The initial benefit of such an exercise is that you better understand the emotions you're experiencing and finding the words to describe them. The follow-on benefits are getting to the cause of that state—to figure out the answer to the question, "Why did I respond this way and not another way?"

Jennifer has been a stay-at-home mom for all of her three children. After her last child departed from home, Jennifer found herself restless, anxious, and unable to concentrate. She became withdrawn from her friends. When around them, she seemed unusually quiet and ill-at-ease.

It's no coincidence that Jennifer began to experience these feelings following her daughter's departure. Her identity and numerous waking hours were spent on raising her children and on her family; now she began to question her purpose in life. She no longer felt camaraderie among many of her friends and began to feel on the outside of their experiences, with little in common. She questioned her ability to connect with other mothers and share the trials and troubles of raising a family. She wondered, "What do I have to share with them?"

How does she begin to define herself without the task of raising her children?

It is common for women to experience some degree of Jennifer's anxiety. Much of her sense of accomplishment and well-being was centered on her children and family. With her children now away, and her free time now abundant, she felt scared and uncertain, not knowing how to begin a new phase of her life.

Before having children she had been a banker, but was now so far removed from the world of finance that it would be difficult for her to return to the career she once knew. Jennifer may have felt like an artist commissioned to paint something rooted in her imagination. She was staring at a blank canvas, not knowing how to begin. She felt that once the painting had begun it was indelible, and unless within the painter's vision, maybe not satisfactory.

While this feeling is common, the reality is quite contrary. Paintings, like life, are a work in progress until they are, in fact, completed. While Jennifer may not know how her life will take shape now, the feelings of anxiety, emptiness, and disorientation may help to catapult her into the next adventure. They are actually useful feelings, because without them, she might try to maintain a status quo and be unable to shift to the next phase of her life.

Starting to Map a Direction Forward

An online search for "empty nest advice" yields more than one million options to gain insights from personal bloggers, television personalities, authors, websites devoted to mental health, and myriad other sources. Rather than duplicate or contradict what they offer, I want to share three types of insights that emerged from stories that may help you map a direction forward. They are about the desire and opportunity to stretch in ways that enable you to feel creative and productive, the renewal and expansion that can come with giving in to your curiosity, and the role of certain habits and rituals in bolstering your sense of equilibrium.

Meredith Vieira, Debbi O'Shea, and Janai Lowenstein are three of the women I have mentioned in this book, in addition to myself, who stretched in new creative directions as part of the Shift. Meredith decided to say "yes" to the offer to do a daytime talk show. Debbi launched her beauty blog. Janai published her first children's book and has others in the works. Regarding my own experience, my agent tells me anecdotally that she believes I have plenty of company in choosing to write a book as my youngest was preparing to leave for college. She noted that just within the past year, she secured contracts for three female clients who had launched, or were about to launch, the youngest child.

For years, even though we may have been working full- or part-time, an abundance of our creative energy and productive moments were invested in our children. The absence of children does not mean that our desire to continue to be creative and productive evaporates; in fact, we might experience a renaissance. With their additional time, the women I just mentioned happened to explore new options in the context of a career. In addition, I heard even more stories about women finding gratifying opportunities through their volunteering.

For the two years immediately after her youngest child left for college, Mary served as president of a charitable organization made up of twenty-four volunteers who raised money to support education opportunities for girls and women. Mary had grown to know the community and its resources well during her years helping to raise money for school programs and the neighborhood teams her children played on. She combined the knowledge she gained from those experiences with a strong desire to use her imagination, skills, and extra time to make a difference with this group. The results astonished everyone; she guided her group into unprecedented fundraising success. She did so well, in fact, that another nonprofit organization in town offered her a full-time job, which she accepted.

Many people talked about finding activities that gave them a sense of renewal and a new dimension in their lives. In my interview with Julia, she mentioned how much she enjoyed reading books about topics that she had always meant to explore, but had never had the time. Happily married for twenty-four years, she was a stay-at-home mom who had devoted full attention to her daughters as they were growing up. When her younger daughter was in her last semester of high school, Julia made a kind of bucket list that contained all the subjects she wanted to learn more about. On her list was fine art. Her reading led her to take a college-level course; that experience made her want to see more original works, so she began driving to the city often to visit museums. Her enjoyment of learning about fine art and her growing appreciation for works of art made her feel as though she were expanding intellectually and emotionally. She was animated about her newfound passion and decided to go back to school and get a degree in the field. The idea thrilled her and she pursued it. On her first day of starting her degree program at the local university, her husband joked that he finally understood what it meant to have an empty nest.

Finding a way forward through the Shift may also involve taking steps to feel comfortable and steady in a period of transition. Earlier in the book, I referred to Leigh, who discovered that setting the table was a ritual that made her feel at home regardless of where she was. Raising an awareness of habits or rituals that provide a sense of continuity and calm can have a great deal of value as you look for new sources of fulfillment and satisfaction. For example, you may have organized your day to be in the car at 3:00 p.m., running an errand, and then picking up your child at school. Perhaps getting in the car at 3:00 p.m. and driving to a yoga class could be a way to keep the same rhythm, yet do something different and fulfilling.

You can't fill all the holes that children and family had filled in your life. Your nest and your life are different. They will never be the same. At the same time, there are countless ways to find opportunities in the time you now have available, and to find satisfaction and resolve as you explore new paths.

THOUGHTS TO CONSIDER

As the departure of your youngest child draws closer, your GPS still has many old maps that reflect the terrain that existed when children populated the home. Updating the maps is a process that begins with a realization that your surroundings are about to change and you want a clearer sense of what lies ahead. At this point, it helps to survey the environment you are in at the moment. The most important factor in that environment is your young adult's readiness to move toward a more independent life. To a great extent, therefore, making choices about your nest and what it will look like day to day is contingent on whether or not the young adult is currently in launch mode.

In this chapter, I looked at the different forms parental support takes, depending on the young adult's pace of progress. As I have mentioned before, every child has unique traits that make it impossible for any book to suggest a precise timeline of when your son or daughter ought to leave home, go to college, or get a job. As you look around at where you are now, try to be objective about what you see and hear. Discussions about college, filling out applications, and other signs of transition mean that change in your nest is imminent. One day your son or daughter goes out the door with packed bags, and you know that change has arrived. On the other hand, if your young adult hesitates to make moves to depart, your choice of where to go next could be profoundly affected by her decision to venture out of the nest incrementally rather than abruptly.

In any case, you might begin to map your direction forward by making a wish list of every possibility that interests you. Rank the items on your list in two ways. First, rank them in terms of actions you can take immediately and options that will take time to explore. On the "now" list, you might have items like taking a class or visiting a place or a person. Then, rank them in terms of appeal. What is your visceral response to "work with the elderly" or "learn French"?

Refine your list based on your responses. You may not have any idea what initial steps you must take to begin working with the elderly, but the thought of embarking on this new activity is exciting. Your curiosity could prompt you to add another short-term action to your list: Do a web search to figure out how you can work with the elderly.

Keep your wish list handy and update it as new ideas occur to you. You are beginning to download the new maps for your GPS and determine a direction forward.

7

POSSIBILITIES

Without leaps of imagination or dreaming, we lose the excitement of possibilities. Dreaming, after all is a form of planning.
                                                    —Gloria Steinem

In her book, *Lots of Candles, Plenty of Cake*, Anna Quindlen
describes how we tend to change our view of, and responses to,
possibilities when we get older. The thirst for novelty and desire to
explore tends to abate and, she concludes, "There comes that moment when we settle down, or settle in, or just settle."[1] But Quindlen does not suggest that's the end of the story, and based on my
interviews and survey data, most of us would agree. After we
launch our young adults into independence, it is likely we will feel
"unsettled" again and morph into an evolved sense of ourselves
with new interests and occupations, if not a new career.

Experiencing a Shift might mean taking a photography class, or
it might mean gardening. One is not innately better than the other—just different. The choice of possibilities depends on the person. Exploring the possibilities you've identified also isn't just
about getting caught up in some activity. In fact, it can be about
not getting caught up. Let me give you a personal example. Early
in our marriage, my husband and I were in our home in a rural

area in upstate Connecticut. Sitting outside with our morning coffee in hand, he said, "Listen."

"Listen to what?" I said. We sat there in silence and then I said, "Oh, there's a bird." A little while later, I heard a gentle breeze moving through the trees. Then I heard rustling in the grass. So with that silence came a symphony of nature.

With quietness comes a heightened perception of your surroundings.

When you attune yourself to that silence in the Shift, you can start to hear sounds in your nest that had previously been drowned out by the noise. Your senses open to possibilities.

Yes, it's true that the rustling in the grass could be a raccoon or it could be a bunny, but if you aren't listening, you won't have any sense of either one being present. Giving yourself time and space to listen means you can not only appreciate the distinct sounds, but also the way they can work together to create a melody.

STEPS TOWARD POSSIBILITIES

Taking the first steps toward new possibilities can occur at different paces for different people. Every person I interviewed described a transition period after the youngest child left home. For some, it was days; for others, it was many months. They described this transition period as a valuable time to move through the emotional changes that naturally come with the Shift. They took inventory of their feelings, interests, relationships, and finances to get some clarity not only about where they were, but also about what kind of future they might have. It was part of the process of getting to know themselves, singularly or as a couple, again.

Their stories surfaced some practical advice about moving forward to examine possibilities in marriage, activities, and personal time. For example, several people noted that right after dropping their son or daughter off at college, they went on a short trip with their spouse. A trip like that doesn't diminish the effect of children being gone, but it helps in setting the stage for the next phase of their life as a couple.

A number of the mothers I spoke with also mentioned that cleaning the young adult's newly vacated bedroom was a cathartic experience. It would be normal to have that activity bring up some feelings of sadness, but the women I spoke with felt it also provided a sense of closure. The room was no longer exactly as it was when their child slept and studied there, and that helped them look forward rather than back.

Several people emphasized the importance of paying more attention to their personal needs as they transitioned to daily life without children at home. Leigh, who was referenced briefly in chapters 3 and 6, went on a yoga retreat for a few days and she came to the significant realization that she could make a home for herself anywhere by setting the table. Emily did an Outward Bound adventure. Janet spent a few days with her mother:

> After settling my youngest daughter into her dorm, I realized I had a lot of unplanned free time. I took advantage of it immediately by driving to my mother's house several hours away. We spent the next three days together shopping, talking, and just sitting together. It was great fun and it took my mind off the fact that my daughter was on her own now.

In the weeks after her youngest son left home, Lisa kept feeling there was a "hole" in her afternoon. She had not had life without the rhythms and demands of children in school for years—and they had been intense years. When her son was entering first grade, she remarried and became a stepmother to two boys, just slightly older than her son. As they grew up together, she had equal involvement in the lives of all three sons.

Lisa had wanted to get back into shape, so one day she went to the gym at 3:30 instead of glancing at the clock and missing her children coming home from school. It then became a daily ritual:

> If I am working out in the gym I go later in the afternoon. Mornings at the gym are filled with the high-energy mothers

who are trying to cram their workout in while their little ones are at school. Not only are the gym and parking lot packed, it is such a clear reminder that I no longer fit into that group. Instead I go in the late afternoon when all the busy moms are doing the school run or afterschool activities with the kids. It keeps me energized and fills the void of my empty house when the boys would be home working on homework, or I would be at their sporting events.

In exploring options during your transition to the resolution stage of the Shift, you might want to consider this tip that Gail Sheehy shares in *New Passages*:

> How do you know where to look for your passion? You can start by seeing if it passes the Time Flies Test. What activity do you do where time goes by without your even knowing it? What did you most love to do when you were 12 years old? . . . Somewhere in that activity there is a hook to be found that might pull up your dormant self.[2]

EXPERIENCING POSSIBILITIES

Of the many people I interviewed, and more than 200 who contributed to my North American survey, the post-launch possibilities they described fell into these categories:

- Pursuing a second career
- Rediscovering a pre-children career
- Reinventing oneself
- Revitalizing their marriage, as if to rediscover a relationship that was kindled prior to children
- Moving on after realizing the marriage/partnership seemed unsustainable without children
- Working to rebuild a problematic marriage
- Establishing an adult relationship with their young adult children

The following stories and insights of how parents faced the post-launch phase of their life may help you to recognize and explore your own possibilities. During this period of discovery and consideration of new options, it might be helpful to look at your opportunities in a variety of ways. The post-launch phase presents unlimited possibilities for personal fulfillment, enrichment, and growth. As you consider the opportunities, you will examine if and how they work within the context of your relationships. With new opportunities come new demands on time and attention. They are among the many moving pieces upon which to reflect when considering a career, volunteer work, hobbies, travel, and other pursuits for self-fulfillment.

Pursuing a Second Career

A second career can refer to one that differs from the professional path that preceded having children or it could refer to a career that follows that of full-time mother. I have an acquaintance who had practiced law prior to the birth of her children. She discovered her second career because of them. Through the years of raising her children, she got a great deal of enjoyment out of planning their parties, and playing games and singing songs with them and their friends. The parties were so successful that other parents began asking her for help planning their children's parties. When her own children grew up and moved out of the family home, doing children's parties became her new career.

Debbi O'Shea (aka DivaDebbi) launched her beauty blog (divadebbi.blogspot.com) when she knew she was three years away from having her son, then a sophomore in high school, depart for college. She describes herself as having been extremely invested in his school, athletics, and life in general. And throughout those years of involvement, Debbi was aware that her situation was a little different from that of the other parents because, among the families in her network of friends, her son was the only "only child." While the other parents would still be going to games and PTA meetings, she and her husband would not.

> We spent so much time with parents—watching games, supporting teams, and doing all of the parent-association activities. That took up chunks and chunks of time, all in a fun and positive way. But I knew that once he left, there would be a gaping hole. I had to take that to heart and figure out how I would fill in some of that time.

She had worked part-time as a personal shopper at Richards of Greenwich while her son was growing up, while organizing her time around his schedule and needs: "He never felt like he had a working mom!" She wondered, after her son left home, what could fill the extra time that would be "fun and satisfying." When she launched the beauty blog, her son was not completely on board with this new activity that was absorbing some of his mother's attention. So Debbi explained *why* she was doing it—her feelings about his eventual leaving, her desire to do something fulfilling and productive, and her joy in using her talents and interests. That was all he needed to throw his support behind her. She admitted to him, "It's not going to be an easy transition for me when you leave."

Debbi's second career reflects a lifelong enjoyment of writing and interest in fashion and beauty trends. But the blog quickly proved to be as much about relationships as fashion and beauty: "It has opened up a whole new network of friends and associates." She soon expanded the reach of her blog to an international audience.

While her choice of blog topics is perfectly consistent with her knowledge and interests, the idea of blogging erupted after she read an article in the *New York Times*:

> On the front page was a story about political bloggers and how they sit in the cafes on Sundays in Washington, D.C. and write their blogs. It's just their personal viewpoint of what's going on. It struck me at that moment what I could do well.

I've always been a girl's girl, always someone who is blasting girlfriends with beauty tips and products I love.

I started the blog that afternoon.

Debbi did not have a lot of technical savvy when she started the blog that Sunday. Her circumstances got her moving and thinking in a different way; they catapulted her to do something she might otherwise not have done. She allowed the challenge to "wake up her brain" in a new way.

Even though Debbi's story is a happy one, she nonetheless went through a brief period of sadness immediately after she and her husband dropped their son off at college. Her words echo the sentiments expressed by parent after parent during interviews and in the survey: "I was in a deep funk for about three days. I sobbed all the way home. The house felt so empty at first." Those feelings are common and they did dissipate, a process helped in large part by her new career.

Debbi's career as a blogger is rich, fulfilling, and applauded by the industry she covers. The DivaDebbi website has received many kudos from prominent colleagues in the arenas of fashion and personal care.

Rediscovering a Pre-Children Career

Kate had been a corporate tax attorney up to the month she gave birth to her first child, and had even published a book on civil rights violations. During the twenty-two years she raised her two boys, she had a career as a decorative artist, allowing her to have flexible hours so she could be a full-time parent as well: "I taught workshops, made beautiful things, and could also be home with the kids."

When her younger son left home, she decided to find out whether corporate tax law was still her calling. "The day he left," she said, "I started working on my resume, doing research, and trying to figure out my next steps." Also just after his departure, she went hiking in a national park with a couple of college girl-friends "to get myself in order." It wasn't that she felt "out of order," but rather that, not having practiced law for more than two decades, she had no confidence in her ability to return.

> I wondered, who will hire me? How do I transition from being a decorative artist and a stay-at-home mom to being a corporate tax lawyer again in a world where the competition is intense? I had to go back to the drawing board to figure out what I had to offer. What was my narrative? How could I speak to the questions of: "Why did I stop?" "Why am I going back?" "What do I bring to the field?" It was challenging.

Kate is a quiet person who, by her own admission, loves to help others, but doesn't feel comfortable asking for help. Nonetheless, she made phone calls to people who could advise her and connect her with opportunities in the field. By October, she had secured a full-time, unpaid position with the same firm she had worked for twenty-two years earlier. She determined that reentering the workforce on an unpaid basis would give her a certain level of comfort—"I could try it on"—and it would make it easier for them to say "yes" to her.

The transition back to law wasn't easy. After a few weeks on the job, she thought about quitting. She thought, "I can't do this." In talking it over with her husband, she quickly realized that if the firm had enough faith in her to give her this opportunity, maybe she should stay at it. She created a self-imposed trial period of three months: "I had to figure out the technology, relearn the language, get used to commuting. It was overwhelming at first."

Within six months, Kate was a paid employee.

Reinventing Oneself

In chapter 3, there was a brief introduction to Leigh, who had a great deal of anxiety over whether or not to leave her marriage after the departure of her children. She felt conflicted over following in her mother's footsteps and sustaining a dysfunctional marriage, or risking the alienation of her children and friends by leaving her own failing marriage.

Leigh decided to leave, with the hope of inventing a new and fulfilling life. All she knew was that she wanted to be engaged in something that allowed her to use her "whole brain." Having been involved in the arts throughout her life, she considered how to turn her interest into a fulfilling and meaningful career.

She had consistently sent a message to her children that, when they grew up, they should be sure to do something that they cared about and to live in a way that honored their values. She did not want her leaving to counter that message. In whatever manner she reinvented herself, she wanted to set a good example for them. Most importantly, she wanted them to always have a sense of being home when they were with her.

With that hope in her heart as well as the possibility of starting a career, she went on a yoga retreat in a monastic environment. Participants there spent much of their time in silence and particularly honored the practice of eating meals in silence. Her first night there, Leigh found a place to sit; she then set the table. It was a practice she always had, even in college. She looked down at the arrangement of the napkin, silverware, and plate and realized, "I've just made a home for myself at this table." Her next thought brought her tremendous relief: Wherever she went, she would set the table and her children would see that and know they were at home with her.

Leigh's young adults did find a home when they came to her apartment for visits, and they also found a mother who was energetically building a meaningful career—something to inspire them as well. In reflecting on her decision to reinvent herself, she said, "When I thought about where I wanted to be when I was young, I'm now where I wanted to be, living the life I'd imagined."

Like Leigh, Carolyn hit a point where she felt her marriage was no longer viable. Rather than wait until her youngest child left, however, she chose to separate from her husband during her daughter's senior year in high school. Her memory of the family home would always be one with children in it; she had effectively, as she said, "frozen the nest in time."

Unlike Leigh, after Carolyn left her marriage, she concluded that she was not living the life she had imagined. She had always envisioned herself as being married and in her family home. Her reinvention came through acceptance that she had to face her new, unimagined world bravely and look for personal satisfaction and growth.

> I always struggled with my work life—or lack of work life—and what kind of contribution I was making. I wondered how to fulfill myself in the world. It plagued me as a mother. I often felt I should be getting a career together. I finally came to the realization that my career was being a mom.

When she was no longer parenting daily, however, Carolyn found her passion: teaching English as a second language. She is figuring out her new career one day at a time, with her struggle now infused with optimism. Reflecting on her life with children and how she might have prepared herself better for her post-launch stage, Carolyn offered this insight: "Just focusing on your children isn't enough. Pay attention to yourself. Pay attention to your marriage."

Revitalizing Their Marriage (Rediscovering a Relationship That Was Kindled Prior to Children)

The early portion of the interview with Julia focused on the anticipation stage of the Shift and on her initial feelings about her youngest daughter's departure. Her days and thoughts seemed consumed by helping her daughter prepare for college.

Post-launch, her husband said something that awakened in her the realization that her focus on the children had made her less available to him: "I feel as though I can have you back now." Julia immediately understood what her husband was saying and was thrilled to know that he was looking forward to the next chapter of their life together. With the children gone, there was much more room for him in her life.

> My husband knows me well. I cried a lot after we dropped off our daughter at college. We made a detour to a camp where we'd been before. We hiked and we swam and we sat around a bonfire. It was a really good in-between thing—social and fun. We didn't want to come right home and he was smart enough to know what would help me start to move past the feeling of emptiness.

Immediately after coming home and seeing her daughter's room, Julia remembers that she and her husband stood still and "sort of stared at each other. If we'd had thought balloons over our head, like in a comic strip, they would have said, 'Who are you?'"

Later that day, they realized the two of them had the time and flexibility to do something spontaneous, so they went out to dinner. It was the first of many dates in their new life together as a couple.

In Nicki's case, it was something her mother said, rather than her husband, that pulled her into the reality that she had new opportunities within her marriage. Married for thirty-two years, Nicki worked in commercial real estate in addition to being a highly involved mother throughout the years her three sons were growing up. She felt knocked off balance after her youngest son moved to college. She had been so involved in the college application process, followed by preparations for attending college, that she admits,

> I was so busy and so hands on—maybe a little too hands on—that I wasn't really aware that he was gone until it happened. I remember coming through my door, walking through the house after we dropped him off, and I thought, I don't want to be at this stage. I knew it was coming, but it was a total shock. I called my mother. She said, "You still have a husband." I can't say I thought of that right away.

Nicki's husband had traveled frequently earlier in his career, but he was starting to have much more time at home just about the time their youngest son entered college. Her mother's blunt reminder helped Nicki immediately awaken to possibilities of using more energy and time for the benefit of her marriage. Making that commitment also helped her ease away from her predisposition to want to talk with her children daily and stay on top of everything that was happening in their lives: "It's not my nature *not* to be involved." When that same level of interest and energy turns toward a marriage, it can have powerful, positive effects.

"Revitalizing a marriage" sounds exciting, but it can also mean a relatively quiet enjoyment of each other. For Jennifer, there were many funny and unexpected signs that she and her husband of thirty-three years were mutually exploring the possibilities of a marriage without their three children:

> At first, I wondered what I would talk to my husband about. Then I realized that we didn't have to talk, and that was fine, too. We could have an intimate and fabulous relationship without a lot of conversation. What I remember thinking before our son left was, "We can go out every night of the week. We can see all the people we didn't have time to see before." I thought we'd be going to the theater all the time and out to dinner.

> What ended up happening was very natural. We would just have food on our laps. Why have a full dinner when all you want is Campbell's soup? It was a different kind of living together. It started to seem more like the life that my grandparents had that I thought was so pathetic, but that wasn't it at all. Watching the evening news in the den with our soup on our laps was fun. Nobody had to cook and we could eat what we liked, even if it wasn't the same thing. There was none of the stress of meal time. If I wanted to have cheese on bread four nights a week I could have it.

Some nights we found ourselves engaged in deep political conversations and other nights we would just sit and pet the dog. No matter what, we still know we love each other.

We realized we didn't have to live up to anyone else's expectations of what that phase in life had to look like or what our actions had to be to find our own happiness and rhythm as a couple. The whole process was actually quite fun.

Jennifer's story reminds me of listening to the symphony of sounds in the quiet countryside that I described early in this chapter. She was able to sit and enjoy the subtle pleasures of her new circumstances. As with many marriages, when the distraction and noise have abated, the quiet gives rise to the harmonious sounds of companionship.

Moving On after Realizing the Marriage/Partnership Seems Unsustainable without Children

Dan and Carrie had been college sweethearts. They married shortly after graduation and started their family the following year. They had two children, eighteen months apart.

Dan had studied architecture, and he pursued his career as Carrie became a full-time mother to their two children. She wasn't sure her degree in English literature would translate into much earning capacity, anyway.

Wanting to spend more time with his son and daughter as they were growing up, Dan left his job with a prominent architecture and engineering firm when the youngest was four years old and set up his own business, running it out of a home office. Carrie welcomed the move. It enabled her to accept a part-time job at a boutique she enjoyed and gave Dan the chance to have more hands-on time with the children. By the time their daughter left for college, the focus of their marriage had become so child-centered, they realized there was little left between them to sustain their marriage. They didn't feel the "glue" anymore.

They sought counseling, but never were able to reconnect with one another. Several years later, they divorced. Dan and Carrie handled it with respect for each other and respect for their children, with both of them creating warm homes for their young adults when they returned for visits and pursuing their own individual paths to build a new future.

Deirdre Bair, author of *Calling It Quits: Late-Life Divorce and Starting Over*, interviewed 126 men and 184 women for her book; all had been married twenty to sixty-plus years when they divorced. One conclusion she came to reflects an important aspect of Dan and Carrie's situation: They considered thoughtfully whether or not divorce was appropriate for them. Bair notes, "Men and women I interviewed insisted they did not divorce foolishly or impulsively. . . . Women and men alike wanted time to find out who they were."[3]

After the breakup of a long-term marriage like the nineteen-year marriage that Carrie and Dan had, many people perceive themselves as young enough to start a new relationship and enjoy many years together with a new partner. For some, remarriage becomes a goal; they want a formalized union and actively seek a partner who desires the same. A growing number of adults ages fifty through sixty-four, however, are choosing to live together and not marry. In 2000, seven percent of adults in that age group were unmarried and living with a partner; by the 2010 U.S. Census, the percentage increased to twelve.[4]

Working to Rebuild a Problematic Marriage

Jane and John had a lot of distance in their marriage. When their youngest daughter left for college, they both seemed to be going their own ways. Jane felt a great deal of frustration because her husband did not understand the loss and loneliness she was experiencing. John was scratching his head, assuming she was simply going through a bad phase in her life because, to him, life seemed the same.

John agreed with her that they needed to improve upon their communication, so they sought therapy. In the sessions, it surfaced that he had a longstanding discontent about not receiving much attention from Jane during the years of raising children. Her primary focus had been on the children and their activities, so he felt like a second-class citizen in his own home. John had always immersed himself in his work and, for years, he let it distract him from the voids in his marriage.

Not unlike John, Jane had compensated for the voids as well. The more John devoted himself to his career, the more consumed she became with being on the front line of meeting their children's daily needs and supporting them in their activities. His pattern continued after their youngest daughter left home; he was not around at home enough to notice a great deal of difference. In contrast, Jane's schedule and focus had a sharp disruption with the departure of their daughter.

Their sense of intimacy had eroded and they both felt disillusioned and disappointed in their marriage. By verbalizing their feelings and identifying the source of their discontent, they were able to discover the frustration, anger, and loneliness they had repressed during the years that work and childrearing schedules had dominated their focus. They came to the realization that blaming and avoiding each other would not allow them to move forward. Through their insights and therapy they were able to reenergize their love and devotion to each other. They discovered that they were both committed to taking time to strengthen their marriage and rebuild their feelings of trust and intimacy.

Establishing an Adult Relationship with Their Young Adult Children

Of all the possibilities discussed in this chapter, this is one that all the parents I interviewed shared. As a result, I have many stories about the process, surprises, and humor of trying to establish an adult relationship with young adult children.

Parents want to enjoy the maturity and expanded interests of their young adults. Christine Proulx, Ph.D., assistant professor of human development and family studies at the University of Missouri, notes, "There are so many joys worth celebrating in this part of life, and my research suggests that watching with pride as the child you've worked so hard to raise matures into an adult is near the top of the list . . . [a related joy is the] possibility to share new things with one's children,"[5] such as education and travel.

In addition to talking with me about the joy of establishing an adult relationship with her own young adults, Meredith Vieira also wove in how pleasant it is to have a relationship with their friends:

> I'm still a parent, but I never imagined how wonderful it would be to sit down with your child, have a glass of wine, talk about what's going on in the world, get their perspective—it's very cool. I'm not saying that now we're best friends. It's still a parent-child relationship, but they're cooked, so to speak. They've got strong opinions—and they care—and I love to hear them express them. And I really love to see their friends, whom I have known since the time they were little. I love to witness what they've become. And it's not surprising. You kind of could have predicted these kids, and they are a delight.

Both in interviews and in the surveys, a number of parents indicated that they had special challenges with "backing off" or "letting go." On a cognitive level, they knew it was time to move toward a more adult relationship with their young adult children; at the same time, they felt emotionally tied to a status quo. In some cases, the challenges of moving toward a more adult relationship related to their parenting style and their young adult's needs. Examples of these would be parenting a young adult with a medical condition such as diabetes or asthma, learning differences, or emotional issues. As I often tell the parents who see me in therapy, "Know your customer!" Some young adults glide into independence, whereas others progress at a slower pace and need ongoing help and encouragement as they move toward maturity.

The impetus for moving toward a more adult relationship with a young adult child reflects many forces at work. Probably the most common experience is that this part of the Shift is organic—it takes shape naturally as both parents and young adult make adjustments in their evolving relationship. Many times the evolution becomes evident when the young adult makes a decision independently that, in the past, would have involved parental input, or even a directive. Decisions regarding how to spend time and what courses to take become the purview of the young adult. In response, the parents' challenge is to avoid judgment (if possible). Use of Socratic questioning can also be helpful, or being neutral rather than reactive and letting the natural consequences of the young adults' choices shape their growth.

Anne made deliberate choices about how to relate to her son during his freshman year of college to help move the relationship to a more adult level. Early in his freshman year, he mentioned in a phone conversation that he had been up partying late a few nights before. Her knee-jerk response was to ask questions that implied disapproval, "Did you get to your classes the next day? Did you get your homework done?" She thought about that and decided to take a different approach the next time that happened. And, of course, it did. In a call a few months later, he said that he and his friends had had a great time staying up until 4 a.m., so he missed his math class the next morning. Anne bit her tongue, wanting him to experience the repercussions of his choices as an adult rather than have "mommy" suggesting what they might be.

There are many variations of Anne's approach. As an executive coach, Barry's profession is to help people increase their self-awareness and communicate more effectively. The skill of coaching came naturally to him; without even thinking about it, he found it helped him in interacting with his teenage son. He found himself adjusting the way he talked with his son as he neared the end of high school. Instead of being directive on a regular basis, he asked more questions. So rather than say, "I don't think you should go out with your friends on a school night," during his son's senior year in high school, he often switched to a question like "Do

you think it's a good idea to go out on a school night?" By the time
his son was in college, the two of them had discussions that were
more adult–to–adult. Barry set the stage for developing a mutual
respect and an evolving adult relationship.

Another part of this journey toward adulthood tends to involve
changes in attitude and behavior. Debbi O'Shea (DivaDebbi) describes her son as "an easy transitioner," who came to appreciate
the new dimension of her life when she launched her beauty blog.
That appreciation was part of the maturing of their relationship.
She says she began to "hover a lot less and give him his space."
When he returns home for visits from college, it strikes her how
their relationship now seems so adult-to-adult:

> He seems to appreciate us more as people than as parents.
> Conversations are more interesting and not as much about him
> and his world, but more about us. We aren't equals, but we
> aren't just mom and dad, either. He no longer brings his phone
> to the table because he knows we will be engaged in conversa-
> tion. He is engaged, focused, and present with us.

Mutuality begins to take shape when both the parent and young
adult see each other in a new light. Shared interests and common
values become clearer to both of them and a new stage of the
relationship starts to evolve.

In summary, what you feel initially is likely to be different from
what you feel down the road, with new interests overtaking those
that seemed to dominate initially. For example, one of the stories
featured earlier in this chapter concerned a woman who returned
to her first career as a lawyer. Three years after she returned to
her field, she left the job. She simply decided to pursue noncareer
interests. This is extremely common, with many people evolving to
a place where they want to spend the remaining productive years
of their life giving back to their community, pursuing a hobby they
never had time for in prior years, traveling, and/or relaxing. In
short, your possibilities in the Shift might change and grow over
time. The options may be endless and may take time to evolve.

The journey is not fixed and may take many circuitous turns before you arrive at the next destination, keeping in mind that there may be more destinations ahead.

THOUGHTS TO CONSIDER

An exciting, hopeful aspect of the Shift is that many people experience a resurgence of their thirst for new adventures and the desire to explore. Throughout this chapter, I shared stories of the kinds of possibilities that parents I interviewed chose to pursue.

To recap, their life after the launch of the youngest child included:

- Pursuing a second career
- Rediscovering a pre-children career
- Reinventing oneself
- Revitalizing their marriage
- Moving on after realizing the marriage/partnership seemed unsustainable without children
- Working to rebuild a problematic marriage
- Establishing an adult relationship with their young adult children

Some of their stories undoubtedly resonated more than others. To begin your personal look at possibilities that represent significant choices about the direction of your life without day-to-day parenting responsibilities, return to the list you made in chapter 6. Expand it with thoughts that the stories may have triggered about your marriage or partnership, career aspirations, volunteer interests, learning opportunities, and new dimensions of your relationship with your children.

Try not to censor yourself. Your long-term dream may have been to sing in an opera and the thought of it still excites you. Pull the item out of your list and give this dream its own page. Fill it with the steps you would need to take to sing in an opera.

As you imagine the possibilities and take action to pursue them, you will see new feathers appearing in your nest. It's highly likely it won't seem empty at all, but rather filled with tangible and intangible signs that you are enjoying the resolution stage of the Shift.

8

RETURN TO THE NEST

Human beings are the only creatures on earth that allow their
children to come back home.
                                    —Bill Cosby, comedian, actor, author

Parenting can be a joy and a job—often, it's both at once. These
two aspects of the parenting experience have been explored in
previous chapters in the context of the Shift. In this chapter, the
emphasis is slightly weighted toward the responsibility side because I explore the feelings and circumstances parents face when
their young adult child cannot make ends meet: They want to help
and, very likely, feel a sense of duty to help. In addition, many
people who thought they were "empty nesters" find themselves
the primary caregivers for their aging parents; they are sandwiched between generations with ongoing responsibilities related
to both. In short, many people after launching their children were
hoping to become what I call *free range parents*, looking forward
to having minimal constraints.

THE ROUND-TRIP

In many instances, young adults initially might not have the income to support themselves and need to return home, which is a reality for a growing number of parents. In her book *The Accordion Family*, sociologist Katherine S. Newman looks at the reality that the number of young adults who are moving back to their parents' home after college is increasing worldwide; she calls it "the private toll of global competition."[1] Pew Research focused on the dramatic increase in the United States alone:

> A Pew Research report earlier this year showed that the share of Americans living in multi-generational households is at its highest since the 1950s. Young adults ages 25 to 34 are most likely to return to the nest. Almost 22 percent of young adults were living at home in 2010, up from 16 percent in 2000 and rising the most since the recession that began in 2007 and technically ended in 2009.[2]

Beth's story is a common one, with her son wondering two weeks prior to graduation from the University of Pennsylvania where he was going to live when he moved out of the dorm. "Am I going to live in Philadelphia?" he asked his mother.

"Not unless you're supporting yourself," she told him. In telling me the story, she laughed: "I thought it was funny that he actually thought we might subsidize him in an apartment when he didn't have a job." That was the first time the subject of where he would live had come up. As a family, they simply had not discussed what would happen after graduation. Beth, her husband, and her son had all formed assumptions that they carried forward. The parents, both of whom worked full-time as journalists, figured he would either get a job and move into an apartment or come home to job hunt. Their son thought his parents might want him to get a place of his own and be out of their hair, regardless of whether or not he could afford it.

Parents like Beth who have had young adults make the round-trip from home to college and back home again offered myriad first responses to the return. Some, like Beth's, are humorous. She said:

> One difficult part of my son coming back was physical: The basement is full of his stuff. As soon as he moved back in, I could hardly get from one end of the basement to the other to do laundry. It's all of his accumulated possessions that will go into an apartment when he moves out. I mostly tolerated his things in the basement because I thought, "Oh, this will just be here a year." The next year, I said to myself, "Oh, this will just be here another year." By the third year, I wanted it to have an expiration date.
>
> Another physical change was that he reverted back to his high school habit of taking over spaces throughout the house. While he was gone, I would come home from work and it was nice to find things in the same place they were when I left the house. When he returned, he would do things like not hang up his coat or take up the dining room table with his things.
>
> As respectful as he is, and as much as he makes contributions to the upkeep of the house, these other physical reminders of his living at home are disconcerting sometimes.

The change Beth describes is really a change in rhythm. The family had gone from triad to dyad, with Beth and her husband establishing a rhythm that involved only the two of them. Their son is productive around the house, and had been very diligent in his job search and in doing part-time work, but the very fact that there was another person in the house disrupted the dyad. The rhythm changed again, going back to what it was before.

Parents like Beth who talked with me about the round-trip had varied perceptions about the unsettling nature of having the nest repopulated by young adults.

Donna talked about the resentment she felt in having to readjust her life. In the years her daughter had been in college, she
had started to build a career. When she returned home, everything went back to the way it was before college. Donna would put
dinner on the table every night, do all the household shopping,
and so on. When she did devote time to her developing career, she
felt guilty about focusing on her work and being gone from the
home so much. Her resentment welled up due to a sense of, "I
shouldn't have to feel guilty about getting on with my life."

Just a few months later, Donna had turned a corner. She said,
"I no longer have the guilt! When she doesn't see me making
preparations for dinner, I sometimes say, 'You're on your own,'
and other times, I ask her to pick up a pizza for us."

A response shared by many is the immediate need to rethink
the rules of the nest. Beth mentioned an interaction with her son
that captures a key issue, that of going out at night. When he first
returned home, she found herself asking what time he would be
home, who he was going out with, what he planned to do—all of
the questions she would have asked when he was in high school.
Her husband suggested she "throttle back" a bit since their son
was now twenty-two and not seventeen.

Another common response is to question whether or not there
will be a return to status quo relating to family life and activities.
In Joan's case, her knee-jerk response was to revert back to the
routine they had prior to her daughter going to college and to
rearrange her schedule in order to make that routine possible.
When Joan recognized that her daughter had begun to demon-
strate more mature young adult behavior, Joan was able to adjust
her parenting to better fit their evolving relationship. It is important to note that this change happened over time. Initially it was
subtle tweaks, ultimately arriving at a comfortable place for everyone. Other parents I spoke with, like Beth, faced a somewhat
easier transition relative to things such as meals and chores because they had worked full-time throughout the years their children were growing up.

In some instances, both parent(s) and young adult have confidence that the move is temporary, and perhaps even a timeline for when the young adult will move out again. There may still be rough spots as the young adult transitions back into life with the parents, but any concerns would likely be mitigated by the fact that there is an end date to the arrangement. For example, the young adult may have received a job offer, but the job won't start immediately so the young adult can't move out until he is earning an income. In *The Accordion Family*, Katherine Newman profiles the Rollo family, in which the parents are delighted to have their son John live at home until he can get into a top graduate school. His goal for a career in humanitarian medical efforts is clear and he's working toward achieving it. The path to building the credentials he needs to get into the school of his choice is an expensive one, yet it is a path that his parents wholeheartedly support. They do not want him to sacrifice his dream by maintaining his own residence.[3]

In situations where there is no sense of exactly when the young adult will move out again, the weeks or months of adjustment may turn into years of adjustment. The natural tendency to return to a status quo conflicts with evolving sensibilities about freedom and control, self-sufficiency and dependence, togetherness and separateness.

Carolyn, whose daughter returned home, told me how impressed she was with how her competence with day-to-day activities grew and took shape throughout the first year she was home again. Without being asked, she took charge of her own laundry, kept her room neat, and did yard work. Carolyn admitted that she had always coddled her daughter because of asthma and allergies, so it surprised her that she seemed to keep moving toward maturity rather than falling back into the dependence she'd had on mother prior to college. On those occasions when Carolyn lapsed into her old coddling style, she noticed "the presence of mommy sucked the competence" out of her daughter. It jarred Carolyn into realizing she had to be consistent in interacting with her daughter as a young adult rather than a child.

Beth's son had been back home for nearly three years when I interviewed her. He had just gotten a job that would enable him to move out, but in the meantime, she had formed quite a few insights about how parents might handle the phenomenon of a round-trip. All of the issues that would generally apply in this situation were present, and they were reminiscent of issues that had been part of the relationship when the son was younger. They included the returning young adult's responsibilities in the household; parameters on his behavior; and expectations of all concerned regarding money, time, and use of space. Specifically, her insights included these thoughts:

- She noted that certain questions or requests, repeated a number of times, will seem like nagging—and that won't move the relationship forward:

  The difficult emotional part was that his dad and I—well meaning as we are—couldn't help but keep saying, "So, how's the job hunt coming?" "How are you doing on that job hunt?" and every other way there is to ask the same question. Needless to say, he perceived it as nagging, which is one of those things that I really tried not to do.

  In a sense, we almost reverted back to the kind of parental positioning that leads to questions like, "Did you do your homework?" Even with the best of intentions, it still sounds like nagging.

- Beth emphasized the importance of acknowledging a job well done, and the value to everyone in the household of having an understanding of who has what responsibilities around the house.

  There were so many things he was able to contribute that it did make up for having the extra body in the house. He painted a couple of our rooms—very professionally—and was diligent with yard work.

His computer died, so to earn the money to pay us back, he did yard work for $15 an hour. He kept up his end of the bargain without fail, paying down the loan on a steady basis.

The chores aspect of his being in the house evolved quickly. He returned home at the end of May and by the end of August, there was a pattern of contribution.

A Pew Research Center survey of young adults between eighteen and thirty-four years old who were living in the parent's home found that 96 percent of them said they did chores around the house. Seventy-five percent indicated they contribute to household expenses and 35 percent pay rent.

- Even as the relationship between parents and young adult kept steadily evolving into an adult-adult relationship, Beth had the sense that her son sometimes appreciated parenting. She said there were times he was glad to have his parents there to advise him about things like career issues, relationship issues, or help with finding housing.
- The final insight is something all parents can use: "In retrospect, I wish we had talked about the financial aspect of growing up a little more specifically as soon as he came back, rather than walk around with our fingers crossed, saying, 'I hope he's doing something to get a job.'"

In all fairness to Beth's son, he was midway through college when the recession hit in 2008. By the time he graduated, young adults were experiencing record-breaking unemployment levels. During the three years he was home, he had a couple of part-time jobs, an apprenticeship, and an internship, all the while sending out resumes and networking. Despite seeing their son engaged in all of those grown-up activities, Beth and her husband could not escape their feeling that their "child" had come home. They experienced their own round-trip. They had begun the journey through the Shift by starting at the anticipation stage before their son was in college, they launched him, and then they settled into a new rhythm when they reached the resolution stage. With their son back home, they went from resolution back to a variation of the initial stage of anticipation.

It was, of course, very different from the first experience. Nonetheless, some of the same feelings were present. Instead of feeling anxious about how their son would fare in college or how they would get through feelings of loss, they were anxious about his ability to find a decent job and keep it so that he could be self-sustaining. They also had feelings of anger and dejection, but not stemming from a sense of emptiness or purposelessness as parents. In this situation, the emotions were directly outwardly toward an inhospitable economic environment that seemed to make it unfairly difficult for their son to start his life as an adult. They also found it upsetting that the economy had put their own lives on hold in certain ways simply because their son was back home and needed their support.

As I write this book, five years have passed since the recession began in 2008. The job market is still extremely challenging for young people, particularly. Articles about young adults returning home are common. *Newsday* reporter Sheryl Nance-Nash looked into the ongoing situation of young adults returning to the nest in a June 23, 2013 article and summarized the advice of several experts on financially coping with the round-trip. She began by citing a survey conducted by Junior Achievement USA and the Allstate Foundation that indicated 25 percent of teenagers said they will likely be twenty-five to twenty-seven years old before becoming financially independent from their parents—an increase of 12 percent from 2011.[4]

The economic downturn that affected families around the world added another level of complexity to the Shift.

THE SANDWICH GENERATION

The financial and emotional stress of having grown children return home is compounded for a growing percentage of people who also provide support to a parent. A 2013 *Wall Street Journal* article called "The Big Squeeze" opened with the sentence: "If you're feeling squeezed these days, blame it on your kids." The article cited a new study called "The Sandwich Generation: Rising Financial Burdens for Middle-Aged Americans" from the Pew Research Center, which concluded:

> Almost half (48 percent) of adults ages 40–59 provided some financial support to at least one grown child in the past year— with 27 percent providing the primary support.
>
> By contrast, 21 percent of adults provided financial support to a parent age 65-plus.[5]

Two years prior to the Pew study, *Forbes* reported that 59 percent of adults in that age range provided some financial support to at least one child, so the number apparently did drop as we saw some small steps toward economic recovery.[6]

The Pew study is insightful for various reasons. It quantifies the extent to which a particular generation faces unusual pressures— and for 41 percent of them, that translates into just barely being able to meet basic expenses or not having enough to meet basic expenses. In addition, it illuminates the fact that this is an issue that touches all economic strata. Looking at the percentage of people who have an older parent and a dependent young adult in terms of household income, nearly half have household incomes that are either below $30,000 or between $30,000 and $100,000.

The Pew study is valuable not merely because of the economic and demographic insights it provides, however. It also illustrates the emotional and practical challenges of having both young adults and aging parents with some level of dependence on the sandwich generation. Fifty-five percent of those who participated in the study said their aging parent *and* grown child relied on them "frequently" or "sometimes" for emotional support. Twelve percent said neither one relied on them for such support, with 23 percent saying it was only the adult child(ren) and 10 percent indicating it was only the aging parent(s).

Some experts believe the toll these ongoing financial and emotional demands take on the "sandwich generation" are serious. The person who coined the term certainly thought so. The phrase "sandwich generation" comes out of a 1981 study by sociologist Dorothy A. Miller, who suggested that those middle-aged adults caught in the middle between two generations have a special need for social services.[7] Miller published her work as life expectancy was steadily rising and at the dawn of a trend toward an increasing number of young adults returning home after college, at least for a short time. Pew's Social and Demographic Trends Project documented that the increase in young adults returning home began in 1980.[8]

The number of people who fit into the category of sandwich generation has grown a great deal since Miller's study; in large part, it's because people are living longer. In 1900, the typical life span in the United States was barely fifty years old. By 2000, it had increased to seventy-six years. By the time she conducted her study, it had already risen to 73.7 years. As of 2011, life expectancy in the United States had risen to 78.57 years, according to the World Health Organization. A complementary statistic from the Journal of Financial Service Professionals makes it even clearer how this affects middle-aged people and gets them "sandwiched": At the dawn of the twentieth century, between 4 percent and 7 percent of people in their sixties had at least one parent living. As of this writing, the figure is up to 50 percent.[9]

In very recent years, media outlets have started to give attention to the need for social services for the sandwiched, such as those Miller addressed in her 1981 study. National Public Radio's "Morning Edition" produced an in-depth series on issues facing the sandwich generation; it was aired in 2012 over the course of eight weeks. Host David Greene emphasized that a key problem is not simply a financial squeeze or emotional demands, but also tremendous fear that their world will fall apart—causing three generations to suffer. The show itself was designed to provide some of the informational services and insights that those who are sandwiched may not be getting from their communities or networks. It covered the psychological trauma of making economic decisions and options for caring for older people, for example.

It's clear we need to do more rather than turn away and assume that providing support for a younger generation and an older generation concurrently is "someone else's problem" resulting from that person's choices. A May 7, 2013 segment of the nationally broadcast Brian Lehrer Show focused on the question, "Why are suicide rates rising for middle-aged adults?" The topic was sparked by a new report from the Centers for Disease Control and Prevention (CDC) stating that more Americans commit suicide than die in car crashes, with an alarming rise in suicides among middle-aged people. One of the significant factors discussed is the squeeze people in this age group are feeling and the overwhelming sense that they just don't have the ability to cope with chronic financial and emotional pressures.

To put sandwich generation issues in the context of the Shift, it is important to acknowledge that some of the new rhythms in the evolving nest can be disrupted by the emerging needs of a parent, just as they were with the return of your young adult. In fact, they will be challenged even if the parent does not actually move in the home, but nevertheless requires steady attention. Caring.com conducted a survey to determine the impact of caring for an aging parent on marriage. Of those middle-aged people who participated, 46 percent said that the caregiving put a strain on their romantic relationship(s). These respondents described a sense of feeling less connected to their spouse or partner; they felt the circumstances were causing them to drift apart.

While many articles written about the survey focused on the negative news, it is important to keep in mind that more than 50 percent of those interviewed apparently did not feel that their romantic relationship was strained. There are varying degrees of dependence that older parents might have, from relying on their children completely for care and financial support to living independently and simply needing occasional assistance with transportation, help around the house, or closer monitoring when they become ill.

Julie told me how much she and her husband enjoy occasionally going on short trips with her elderly parents, who are no longer physically able to travel by themselves. By handling all the logistics and accompanying them, Julie and her husband make it possible for her parents to continue to take vacations and fly to family reunions. Julie has a grown son who decided to take a year off from college and live at home until he's more certain of his career path. The short trips that Julie and her husband take with her parents give everyone a break from the repopulated nest. In this case, being "sandwiched" is a positive experience.

Adding another generation to the home is potentially a more stressful situation than occasional caregiving, of course. It may not only put strains on a marriage, but it may also bring up parenting issues. Much of the Shift is about transitions in your parenting style as your young adult moves toward complete independence. Having parental input from a senior member of the family could disrupt that rhythm as well.

Having three generations in a household is not all about disruption of rhythms or stress, however. It is also about emotional bonds and opportunities for generations to connect in a new way. When people feel as though they have places where they can enjoy privacy, a clear understanding of who does what in the house, and respect for possessions and preferences, the multigenerational arrangement can be a positive experience.

Whether or not the parent requiring some care moves into the home, it's important to be aware of certain aspects of the relationship that can be challenging for all concerned. The older person is experiencing diminished self-sufficiency and autonomy, whereas the younger people around her probably still have a relatively quick pace and the energy to get more things done in a day. What the older person might have done in the past stress-free, she now sees as a daunting task. Taking back a product that's defective or making a medical appointment might require more energy than the older person has at the moment; that can create frustration and anxiety for her. In turn, the middle-aged adults who are trying to be loving, helpful, and attentive might find it jarring to see their parent having difficulty with day-to-day tasks. They take a level of energy, ability, and confidence for granted and they may become uncomfortable or even impatient with a slower-moving older person who seems tentative much of the time. There are a lot more moving pieces with a person of the older generation than with younger people. In other words, younger people might see a doctor's appointment as a single activity, whereas an older person thinks about it as eight activities: getting dressed to go out, calling a cab, paying the driver, waiting in the doctor's office, going through the examination, getting a cab to go home, paying the driver, and sitting down to rest after all the disruption.

This is very reminiscent of how it was when our children were young. They required managing as well as consistency in their world. The status quo is comforting for the elderly, just as it's comforting for a child. Older people tend to feel changes much more intensely than younger adults. Part of the Shift, then, may well involve being a much bigger part of a parent's life, regardless of whether or not the parent is in the same residence.

Despite the similarities between parenting a child and helping an older adult, it's important to remember not to parent your parents. My mother drives, but when she goes out at night, she has someone else drive her. I recently went out to dinner with my husband prior to my mother going out for the evening and, as we were driving to the restaurant, I thought, "I forgot to ask my mother if she made plans for someone to drive her tonight!" I decided not to act on the thought, however, because my mother probably would not have appreciated a call from me "checking up on her" about her plans.

The key concept for the sandwich generation to keep in mind in trying to achieve a positive experience is balance. We have to find a balance between respecting the older generation—not diminishing their capabilities—and providing practical and emotional support in ways they need and want it. Likewise, we have to balance between respecting our young adult's need for autonomy and providing continuing guidance on responsibilities and behavior.

The Shift is a 360-degree experience, impacting every area of one's life. Regardless of what the demands are on you, maintaining a balance of making space for yourself while handling the additional responsibilities of being sandwiched is essential. The Shift is a journey with many challenges and surprises along the way.

The opportunity of being sandwiched can redefine and reinvigorate your relationships with both the young adults and the older adults in your family. At the same time, however, you may also have a marriage or partnership or other important relationships that you want to nurture. Connecting with others, as well as taking time for yourself, is a juggling act—and you may drop a ball or two occasionally. Pick it up when you can and keep moving. The Shift and all of its aspects is a work in progress.

THOUGHTS TO CONSIDER

In this final chapter, I examined the Shift in the context of young adults returning to the nest and parents or other older relatives needing caregiving on a regular basis. Your process for pursuing your own opportunities for personal or professional growth and development can seem challenged under those circumstances. However, with an open and flexible mindset, what could be viewed as interruptions and obstacles might instead be considered meaningful opportunities to develop new dimensions of your relationships with the maturing members of your family.

An increasing number of people who thought they were "empty nesters" find themselves with a young adult who has made the round-trip and/or they become the primary caregivers for their aging parents. Sandwiched between generations, they have ongoing responsibilities related to both. Instead of becoming "free-range parents," looking forward to having minimal constraints, they have to rethink their timeline for travel, hobbies, and the pursuit of other interests.

Again, people will experience this differently. For some, a return to the role of caregiver is a welcome relief, the comfort of which stems from its familiarity. On the other hand, some might feel that their transition into a new exciting phase has been squelched. The latter group will have to recalibrate their expectations to fit their circumstances. There are strategies for adjusting expectations that involve not only you, but also those between whom you feel sandwiched. Objectives that these strategies must address include your own need for balance and your rekindled interest in your own development.

For example, if a young adult has returned home, find out what your son's or daughter's thoughts are about the timetable for finding a job and new living situation—fundamentals to independence. What does your young adult think is reasonable? You are not asking for a promise, but rather a perspective. Share your thoughts about what you think is reasonable. The discussion on the topic of a timeline should not have a punitive edge. This is not about a punishment or an ultimatum. You simply need some collaborative efforts and shared ideas of both parents and the young adult about further developing his or her independence.

In the meantime, it is important for you to set guidelines and limits. Even though your returning son or daughter may yet to have established financial independence, your expectations as to what and how your young adult contributes must be clearly defined and articulated.

Define the terms of your young adult's responsibilities for bill paying, household chores, and other types of positive involvement at home. This clarity fosters the continued evolution of your nest while promoting your young adult's autonomy.

Setting realistic expectations may also mean they need assistance in learning to budget and/or manage time and money. Based on your young adult's skill sets, figure out what you can do together to ease the pressure and stresses of the round-trip arrangements with attention to striking a balance between supporting and enabling.

If you are sandwiched between generations, the emotional, financial, and time pressures might seem overwhelming, if not smothering. The now-doubled stress and concern of caregiving can easily rob a person of perspective on what is reasonable, or even healthy, under the circumstances.

It is therefore critical to understand clearly your own capabilities and limitations. Make a list of needs for which you require assistance, or want assistance. Next, explore the community programs, aging parent support groups, churches, synagogues, and hospitals that can address the needs you've listed. Hang up your Superman cape. Caring for your own emotional, practical, and financial needs enables you to do a better job of addressing those of the older people who need your help.

While the round-trip and sandwich generation responsibilities both impact the refeathering of your nest, they do not have to stop the process. You might want to do it all, but acting on that want is neither healthy for you nor optimal for those who depend on you. Communicate and collaborate with your young adult who has returned. Seek assistance to help you with your parents who need your care. These strategies will allow you to continue the Shift and the process of refeathering your nest.

CONCLUSION

In the beginning of the book, I told you I threw away my son's high school calendar just after he graduated. It was a moment when, on a conscious level, I recognized that our nest was evolving. The year that followed contained many other such moments, some more protracted than others and some more remarkable than others. Moving him into the dorm, having him home for a holiday, not having either of my sons at a family gathering—it was times such as those when the Shift was not only an emotional, but also a cognitive, process.

When my younger son returned to college for his sophomore year, I helped him move into his first apartment with a couple of friends. As we put pots and pans into kitchen cabinets and a rug on the bathroom floor, I was aware of the fact that I was helping him build his own nest. I was with my young adult in a new place, filled with furnishings that he chose—a place that, at least while in college, he would refer to as "home." At the same time, many parents were helping their young adults settle into dorms and apartments in the area. Stores were crowded with young adults and their parents planning for a new living situation. We all had a similar mission of helping our young adults further transition to greater independence.

In the midst of all the many launch activities, discussions of the Shift seemed prevalent everywhere—cocktail parties, workplace, gym. Without question, I often felt I had a great deal of company in the journey. The statistics on so-called empty nesters reinforced my desire to write this book: Roughly 25 million people of my generation were going through the Shift at the same time. Even the president of the United States has joined in the collective consciousness about transitioning to home life without children. When President Barack Obama and First Lady Michelle Obama got a one-year-old puppy in August 2013, the president remarked, "I think there is an element for Michelle and me of, you know, we see what's coming and we need to make sure that we got some-body who greets us at the door when we get home."[1]

One point that I have tried to illuminate throughout the book is that the Shift does have a cognitive element—we are thinking through what's happening—but it is equally important to recog-nize the emotional effects. Hints, or even waves, of emptiness may accompany our awareness of the changes. A moment later, we might realize that we don't have to have dinner ready at a specific time, we can go out spontaneously to a movie with friends, or plan a weekend trip. The emotional fluctuations may be unlike any-thing we have experienced in decades.

While the preponderance of insights in this book are about the parents' emotional transitions and experiences in the Shift, I also want to give some additional attention to what young adults are feeling. As they adjust to changing environments and relation-ships, their behavior might seem inscrutable to the parents at times. The young adults are sometimes floundering as they navi-gate an important phase of life.

The young adults may have fear of the unknown as they pre-pare to enter an unfamiliar environment filled with human and logistical variables. At times, they may feel sad about leaving close friends and family. Even though they are still young adults, they may also have some nostalgia or feeling of loss about the "good old days" when they played soccer on the championship high school team or had a major role in the senior class play. They are also likely to have uncertainty about moving away from a home and community that are familiar and offer support systems, as well as leaving behind comforting routines that were part of their lives for years. Along with those feelings, they probably have a sense of pride and optimism about soon establishing routines of their own design. In that sense, they are leading change. At the same time, they are still not completely independent. The parents are still involved, striving to evolve their parenting. While promoting the young adult's exercise of autonomy, at the same time they are offering parental guidance that may be perceived by the young adult as reminiscent of when they were younger. That kind of dynamic between the evolving young adult and the evolving parent could easily set the stage for tension in the home. It may even give rise to a kind of defiance in young adults that surfaces as a push-pull relationship they have with the status quo at home and, perhaps even with their parents.

With all of the changes going on just before, during, and after the launch, neither parent nor young adult can be expected to be consistently balanced and mindful of each others' feelings. Perhaps the most practical goal to aim for is raising the level of awareness of the various challenges, expectations, and emotions of everyone in the household. Raising such awareness is one of the goals of this book.

Hopefully, the previous chapters have also shed light on how distinctly many aspects of parenting have changed since the World War II generation raised the baby boomers, with the changes relating to both women and men. Women commonly have focused on building a career in their twenties, and either postponing or choosing not to raise children. Those who postponed parenting often went into it with a strong sense of planning and meticulous attention to parenting with precision. At the same time, an increasing number of men have become active fathers, trying to rearrange schedules to attend games and PTA meetings. Starting with the baby boomer generation, many single parents and couples became what I call precision parents.

In talking with people who are on the outside looking in—that is, men and women of an earlier generation or perhaps those who chose not to be parents—their thoughts of how parents today would respond to launching their children is often antithetical to the reality of precision parents. It seems that at least some thought it would be relatively easy for us to adjust to an evolving nest. We could simply replace parenting with a career renaissance, travel, hobbies, or volunteerism. In short, since we had active lives that were more self-focused prior to parenting, we could essentially just pick up where we left off.

Parents going through the Shift understand the irony of that supposition. Parenting became our career, regardless of whether or not we worked outside the home. Having wholeheartedly invested our time, resources, and emotional and intellectual energy in parenting, it's only natural to have an acute sense of loss when the daily requirements of parenting end. Simply stated, we miss it, and there is no substitute for it; however, missing it doesn't preclude us from growing and evolving. While life will never be the same, it still can be enriching and your relationship to children and family can progress in a whole new dimension.

A number of people I interviewed said specifically that one of the unexpected joys of this new phase of life was getting to know their children's friends, as well as their own young adults, on an adult level. Hearing their insights about everything from dating to politics is fun and it's gratifying. You spend decades of your life bringing them along emotionally, intellectually, and socially, and then at some point, experience this great reward of having them share with you the ideas they've forged and the knowledge they've accumulated.

Adjusting to daily life without children is a fact of life and part of a process, but not a "syndrome." Another key message running throughout this book is that "empty nest syndrome" does not exist. The medical definition of a syndrome is this: "a group of signs and symptoms that occur together and characterize a particular abnormality."[2] As a psychotherapist, I can assure you that the collective experiences associated with launching your children are typical rather than abnormal. A compelling reason for me to write this book is to explore the fact that the evolving nest is related to a life phase with three main stages—the Shift—rather than a syndrome. The different phases may involve some acute emotions, yet they are a common and expected part of the changes in your nest. During the Shift, your relationships and routines are moving pieces; your expectations and feelings are in flux. "Empty nest syndrome" does not adequately capture the dynamic nature of what's occurring in your life.

After reading this book, hopefully you will have a better understanding of the evolving nest and its impact on you and others around you. Thinking in terms of anticipation, launch, and resolution—the stages of the Shift—will hopefully help you stay mindful that you are going through changes rather than stuck in a "syndrome." The concept of the Shift embodies a sense of movement, transformation, and possibilities.

Because the Shift is a phase of life, like any other life phase, it's fluid, unpredictable, and different from person to person. As a corollary, no two nests will evolve in the same way as their occupants go through the Shift. There is another corollary as well: When grown children move back to the home and/or the older generation of parents move into the home, one or more of the stages of the Shift could very well repeat.

According to Pew Research on Social and Demographic Trends, more than 51 million Americans live in a multigenerational household. These households included one-in-six Americans (16.7 percent) and more than one-in-five (21.1 percent) adults ages twenty-five to thirty-four.[3] This means that many people who thought they moved well into the resolution stage of the Shift may find themselves relaunching the boomerang generation—that is, young adults who have left home and then returned to live in their parents' home. At the same time, perhaps some of the possibilities they began to explore, such as a new career or travel, might have to be put on hold because aging parents need regular care.

Even though stages of the Shift may repeat due to such circumstances, the experiences aren't likely to feel exactly the same the second time around. The same description I gave the Shift earlier still applies: It's largely unpredictable as well as fluid.

Perhaps the one aspect of it where there is some certainty is that we return to the nest, at least for awhile. It's the place we have called home with our children and, regardless of where we might go next, it will always carry that significance.

Three weeks before my younger son would be leaving for his sophomore year in college, I noticed a bird was building a nest near the house. I got the binoculars, but couldn't see if there were eggs in the nest. It was late in the year for birds to be nesting in the Northeast, so I was very curious about the behavior. Then one day I noticed that the bird was flitting back and forth all day long, working away; then I heard chirping. It wasn't a chorus, but just a single tiny bird peeping loudly. I saw the mother come and feed it, and then later saw it flapping around. About a week later, the nest was empty. No one ever came back to the nest.

Like the birds, humans are very goal-directed in nurturing our young. Unlike the birds, we still want to come back to the nest after our young leave it. It isn't just a place for having and raising little ones; it's a place we can call home—with or without them. We still want to make the nest comfortable for ourselves.

What I have tried to do in this book is present you with stories that remind you of how much company you have in your journey, as well as an array of ideas about what possibilities might lie ahead for you. As you set about refeathering your nest, always remember that it's *yours* and no one outside of it can really know which feathers belong there. Hopefully, you will be patient with yourself as you choose those feathers—it can take time—and know that your choices may change in the very near future.

GLOSSARY

accordion family—A term popularized by Johns Hopkins University sociologist Katherine Newman to describe families that have young adults who previously departed the home returning due to economic constraints

anticipation stage—The stage of the Shift prior to launch (See also "launch stage" and "Shift, the")

Boomerang generation—One term used to describe the millennial generation (aka Generation Y, born between the late 1980s and early 2000s), which faced such a severe economic downturn during job-hunting and early career years that many young people returned home, or "boomeranged" back to the nest

free range parents—Parents with reduced constraints due to having launched all their children.

gap-year program—A period of time when students take a break from formal education; gap-year programs generally involve travel, volunteering, alternative studies, internships, or work

helicopter parent—A term first used in a 1990 book by Foster Cline and Jim Fay and popularized in the twenty-first century, it refers to a "hovering" style involving intense parental support of various kinds, including academic, financial, emotional, and social

launch stage—The stage of the Shift characterized by the departure of the young adult from the nest (See also, "Shift, the")

parallel process—Concurrently aiming to achieve two objectives; in the context of the evolving nest, it refers to a dynamic such as the following: While the parents are teaching their young adult to think independently, they are helping themselves to let go and to move toward redefining their relationship so it's more balanced.

precision parent—A term coined by Wendy Aronsson to describe parenting evolved by baby boomers that is purposeful, mindful, and deliberate, reflecting the kind of focus on parenting that is often associated with careers

psychotherapy—Refers to therapeutic interaction between a trained professional and an individual, couple, family, or group

resolution stage—The stage of the Shift that is post-launch and involves parents coming to terms with the fact that they no longer have day-to-day parenting responsibilities (See also "launch stage" and "Shift, the")

round-trip—A way of describing the return of a launched young adult to the nest

sandwich generation—Any generation that cares for aging parents while supporting their own children

Shift, the—A term coined by Wendy Aronsson to describe a life phase revolving around the departure of young adults from the nest

NOTES

1. PARENTING IN THE EVOLVING NEST

1. Projection extrapolated from the Datamonitor survey, "Empty nesters and financial services," June 2005.

2. 2004 Del Webb Baby Boomer Survey, http://dwboomersurvey.com/.

3. Robert A. Lewis, Phillip J. Freneau, and Craig L. Roberts, "Fathers and the postparental transition," *The Family Coordinator*, Vol. 28, No. 4.

4. Rebecca A. Clay, "An empty nest can promote freedom, improved relationships," *Monitor on Psychology* (American Psychological Association), Vol. 34, No. 4, p. 40, April 2003.

5. From www.amazon.com, October 2012.

6. Anna Freud, *Normality and Pathology in Childhood: Assessments of Development*, Karnac Books, 1989.

7. Mary D. Salter Ainsworth, Mary C. Blehar, Everett Waters, and Sally Wall, *Patterns of Attachment: A Psychological Study of the Strange Situation* (Hillsdale, NJ: Lawrence Erlbaum Associates, 1978).

8. Simon Baron-Cohen, Alan M. Leslie, and Uta Frith, "Does the autistic child have a 'theory of mind'?" *Cognition*, Vol. 21, pp. 37–46, 1985.

9. Kevin Liptak, "Preparing to be 'empty nesters,' the Obamas turn to Sunny," August 23, 2013, http://politicalticker.blogs.cnn.com/2013/08/23/preparing-to-be-empty-nesters-the-obamas-turn-to-sunny/.

10. The Moral Lives of Children Project, "The Culture of American Families," University of Virginia's Institute for Advanced Studies in Culture study, http://iasc-culture.org/research_character_of_american_families_project.php.

11. Shriram Harod, "Boomer parents optimistic about kids' prospects, despite continued financial dependence," Huffington Post, June 22, 2010, http://www.huffingtonpost.com/2010/04/22/boomer-parents-optimistic_n_546988.html.

12. Foster W. Cline and Jim Fay, *Parenting with Love and Logic: Teaching Children Responsibility* (Colorado Springs, CO: Piñon Press, 1990), 23–25.

13. K. L. Fingerman, Y.-P. Cheng, E. D. Wesselmann, S. Zarit, F. Furstenberg, and K. S. Birditt, "Helicopter parents and landing pad kids: Intense parental support of grown children," *Journal of Marriage and Family,* Vol. 74, No. 4, 880–96, August 2012.

14. Sindya N. Bhanoo, "For hummingbirds, it's easy to shift into reverse," *The New York Times*, October 1, 2012, http://www.nytimes.com/2012/10/02/science/for-hummingbirds-its-easy-to-shift-into-reverse.html?_r=0.

15. http://digitaljournal.com/article/314554.

2. STAGES OF THE SHIFT

1. Elisabeth Kübler-Ross, MD, *On Death and Dying* (New York: Scribner, 1969).

2. Sara Lipka, "Helicopter parents help students, survey finds," *Chronicle of Higher Education,* Vol. 54, No. 11, p. A1, Nov. 2007. The title reference is to a 2007 study of the National Survey of Student Engagement that found that helicopter parents may actually help students thrive.

3. E. H. Erikson, *Identity: Youth and Crisis* (New York: W.W. Norton, 1968).

4. M. Solomon, "A developmental conceptual premise for family therapy," *Family Process*, Vol. 12, No. 2, pp. 179–88, 1973.

5. The earliest reference to "empty nest syndrome" appears to be in a study by Eva Y. Deykin, Shirley Jacobson, Maida Solomon, and Gerald Klerman called, "The empty nest: Psychosocial aspects of conflict between depressed women and their grown children," *American Journal of Psychiatry*, Vol. 122, pp. 1422–26, June 1966.

6. University of Missouri-Columbia, "Empty nest syndrome may not be bad after all, study finds," *ScienceDaily*, February 24, 2008. Retrieved from http://www.sciencedaily.com /releases/2008/02/080221133313.htm.

7. Kübler-Ross, *On Death and Dying*, p. 52.

8. Ibid, p. 64

9. Louann Brizendine, MD, *The Female Brain* (New York: Morgan Books, 2006), p. 95.

10. Ellen J. Langer, *Counterclockwise: Mindful Health and the Power of Possibility* (New York: Ballantine Books, 2009), p. 74.

11. Sandy Cohen, "Woodard dives into work to cope with empty nest," The Associated Press, September 18, 2012, http://www.adn.com/ 2012/09/18/2630112_woodard-dives-into-work-to-cope.html.

12. Kübler-Ross, *On Death and Dying*, p. 124.

13. From an interview with Gina Shaw, "Kyra Sedgwick on work, family, and empty nests," *WebMD Magazine*, 2012.

3. THE ROLE OF PERSONAL EXPERIENCE

1. www.mayoclinic.com/health/empty-nest-syndrome/MY01976.

2. Sarah Smiley, "Changing gender roles mean new sacrifices for military fathers," *Bangor Daily News*, June 16, 2013, http:// bangordailynews.com/2013/06/16/living/blogs-and-columns-living/ changing-gender-roles-mean-new-sacrifices-for-military-fathers/.

3. Rosalind Barnett, Nancy Marshall, and Joseph Pleck, "Study of full-time employed dual earner couples," *Journal of Marriage and the Family* (1992), Vol. 54, pp. 358–67.

4. Gail Sheehy, *New Passages* (New York: Random House, 1995), p. 281.

5. Deborah Rozman, "Managing empty-nester stress," Huffpost Healthy Living, July 6, 2013, http://www.huffingtonpost.com/heartmath-llc/empty-nester-stress_b_3529454.html.

6. Cori Linder, from an interview with Tammy Hotenspiller, "Helpful tips for empty nest moms," Modern Mom Parenting, http://www. modernmom.com/blogs/cori-linder/helpful-tips-for-empty-nest-moms.

7. Greg Baker, "The relationship between fear and anger," Yahoo!, June 10, 2011, http://voices.yahoo.com/the-relationship-between-fear-anger-8619049.html?cat=41.

8. Linda Walter, "Living without anxiety," *Psychology Today*, August 14, 2011, http://www.psychologytoday.com/blog/life-without-anxiety/201108/fear-or-not-fear-you-re-in-control.

9. http://www.ziplinelady.com/2012/08/the-fullness-of-an-empty-nest/.

10. Megan Ray, "Coping with empty nest syndrome," Sunrise Senior Living Blog, July 9, 2013, http://www.sunriseseniorliving.com/blog/july-2013/coping-with-empty-nest-syndrome.aspx.

11. From The Free Online Dictionary, http://www.thefreedictionary.com/Reframing.

12. From an interview with Meredith Vieira conducted on July 16, 2013.

13. Ibid.

4. LOOKING INSIDE THE NEST

1. Barbara Rainey and Susan Yates, "Three pitfalls to avoid in an empty nest marriage," Family Life, http://www.familylife.com/articles/topics/marriage/challenges/empty-nest-and-midlife/three-pitfalls-to-avoid-in-an-empty-nest-marriage#.Uipu8sasj2w.

2. Sara M. Gorchoff, Oliver P. John, and Ravenna Helson, "Contextualizing change in marital satisfaction during middle age: An 18-year longitudinal study," *Psychological Science*, Vol. 19, No. 11, pp. 1194–1200, November 2008.

3. Tara Parker-Pope, "Your nest is empty? Enjoy each other," *New York Times*, January 19, 2009.

4. David Heitman, "At random: Summer offers neat peek at empty nest," *The Advocate*, July 13, 2013, http://www.nytimes.com/2009/01/20/health/20well.html?_r=0http://theadvocate.com/features/people/6313844-123/at-random-summer-offers-neat.

5. Michael Bogdanow, "The ups and downs of empty nesting," *The Safety Report*, June 24, 2013, http://thesafetyreport.com/2013/06/the-ups-and-downs-of-empty-nesting/.

6. Susan Brown and I-Fen Lin, *The Gray Divorce Revolution: Rising Divorce among Middle-aged and Older Adults, 1990–2009*.

7. From an interview with Susan Brown on "Talk of the Nation," National Public Radio, March 8, 2012, http://www.npr.org/2012/03/08/148235385/gray-divorce-over-50-and-splitting-up.

8. "AARP the magazine study on divorce finds that women are doing the walking—but both sexes are reaping rewards in the bedroom," May 2004, http://www.aarp.org/relationships/love-sex/info-2004/divorce.html.

9. Deirdre Bair, "The 40-year itch," *New York Times*, June 3, 2010.

10. Susan Gregory quoting Betsey Stevenson in "The gray divorcés," *Wall Street Journal*, August 28, 2012.

11. Arland Thornton and Linda Young-DeMarco, "Four decades of trends in attitudes toward family issues in the United States: The 1960s through the 1990s," *Journal of Marriage and Family*, Vol. 63, No. 4, pp. 1009–37, November 2001, http://onlinelibrary.wiley.com/doi/10.1111/j.1741-3737.2001.01009.x/abstract;jsessionid=AAEF082FDD76879979F77FA64F2AB9C3.d02t03?deniedAccessCustomisedMessage=&userIsAuthenticated=false.

12. Ibid.

13. Jim McCormick, primary research done to support *The Power of Risk* (Maxwell Press, 2008).

14. Gail Sheehy, *New Passages* (New York: Random House, 1995), p. 9.

15. Ibid., p. 140.

16. Orna Gadish, MSC, *Don't Say I Do!*, New Horizon Press, 2012, p. 95.

17. Calculated from U.S. Bureau of the Census (2000).

5. REMINISCING ABOUT YOUR PARENTING

1. Anita Hofschneider, "Hiring millennials? Meet the parents?," *Wall Street Journal*, September 11, 2013, B6.

2. Ibid.

3. Ibid.

4. Madeline Levine, "Raising successful children," *New York Times*, August 4, 2012.

5. Norman E. Rosenthal, from a review of *The Gift of Adversity* by Jane E. Brody, "Life's hard lessons," *New York Times*, September 9, 2013, http://well.blogs.nytimes.com/2013/09/09/lifes-hard-lessons/?_r=0.

6. Susan Engel, "When they're grown, the real pain begins," *New York Times*, November 28, 2012, http://www.nytimes.com/2012/11/28/booming/when-theyre-grown-the-real-pain-begins.html.

7. Ibid.

8. Pew Internet and American Life Project, "Teens, smartphones and texting," Pew Research Center, March 19, 2012, p. 2.

9. Katherine Shulten, "Do you have helicopter parents," *New York Times*, May 14, 2013, http://learning.blogs.nytimes.com/2013/05/14/do-you-have-helicopter-parents/?_r=0.

10. Ibid.

6. CHALLENGES, UNCERTAINTIES, FEAR

1. Peter Spevak and Maryann Karinch, *Empowering Underachievers* (Revised and Expanded Edition), New Horizon Press, 2006, p. 5.

2. StudentAwards.com, "Gap year—thinking outside the box," http://www.studentawards.com/stacks/articles/gap-year-thinking-outside-the-box.aspx.

3. Mary Tuggle Payne, "Not quite ready for college at 17," Better After 50, April 3, 2013, http://betterafter50.com/2013/04/not-quite-ready-for-college-at-17/.

4. Email from Janai Lowenstein, July 28, 2013.

7. POSSIBILITIES

1. Anna Quindlen, *Lots of Candles, Plenty of Cake* (New York: Random House, 2012), p. 117.

2. Gail Sheehy, *New Passages: Mapping Your Life across Time* (New York: Random House, 1995), p. 153.

3. Deirdre Bair, "The 40-year itch," *New York Times*, June 3, 2010.

4. Rachel L. Swarns, "More Americans rejecting marriage in 50s and beyond," *New York Times*, May 2012, p. A14.

5. http://life.gaiam.com/article/empty-nest-doesnt-have-mean-emptiness.

8. RETURN TO THE NEST

1. Katherine S. Newman, *The Accordion Family: Boomerang Kids, Anxious Parents, and the Private Toll of Global Competition* (Boston: Beacon Press, 2012).

2. *USA Today*, October 16, 2012.

3. Newman, *Accordion Family*, pp. xv–xvii.

4. Sheryl Nance-Nash, "Not-so-empty nest: Set boundaries when kids return," *Newsday*, June 23, 2013.

5. Journal Reports, "The Big Squeeze," *Wall Street Journal*, March 18, 2013.

6. Jenna Goudreau, "Nearly 60% of parents provide financial support to adult children," *Forbes*, May 20, 2011.

7. Dorothy A. Miller, "The 'sandwich' generation: adult children of the aging," *Social Work*, Vol. 26, No. 5, pp. 419–23, September 1981.

8. http://www.pbs.org/newshour/rundown/2012/03/pew-study-young-adults-ok-with-moving-back-home-1.html.

9. http://seniorliving.about.com/od/babyboomers/a/sandwich-generation.htm.

CONCLUSION

1. "Puppy fills gap left by busy teenagers in Obama White House," Reuters, August 23, 2013, http://news.yahoo.com/puppy-fills-gap-left-busy-teenagers-obama-white-155203319.html.

2. http://www.merriam-webster.com/medical/syndrome.

3. Rakesh Kochhar and D'Vera Cohn, "Fighting poverty in a bad economy, Americans move in with relatives," Pew Research Center, October 3, 2011, http://www.pewsocialtrends.org/2011/10/03/fighting-poverty-in-a-bad-economy-americans-move-in-with-relatives/4/.

BIBLIOGRAPHY

Arp, David H., Arp, Claudia S., Stanley, Scott M., Markman, Howard J., and Blumberg, Susan L. (2001). *Empty Nesting: Reinventing Your Marriage When the Kids Leave Home*. San Francisco: Jossey-Bass.

Bertini, Kristine. (2011). *Strength for the Sandwich Generation: Help to Thrive While Simultaneously Caring for Our Kids and Our Aging Parents*. Santa Barbara, CA: Praeger.

Chapman, Gary D., and Campbell, Ross, M.D. (2011). *How to Really Love Your Adult Child: Building a Healthy Relationship in a Changing World*. Chicago: Northfield.

Coburn, Karen Levin, and Treeger, Madge Lawrence. (2009). *Letting Go: A Parents' Guide to Understanding the College Years Paperback* (5th ed.). New York: Harper Perennial.

Konstam, Varda. (2013). *Parenting Your Emerging Adult: Launching Kids from 18 to 29*. Far Hills, NJ: New Horizon Press.

Newman, Katherine S. (2012). *The Accordion Family: Boomerang Kids, Anxious Parents, and the Private Toll of Global Competition*. Boston: Beacon Press.

Quindlen, Anna. (2013). *Lots of Candles, Plenty of Cake*. New York: Random House.

Sheehy, Gail. (1995). *New Passages: Mapping Your Life Across Time*. New York: Random House.

INDEX

ABOUT THE AUTHOR

Wendy Aronsson, LCSW, has been a licensed psychotherapist since 1981 and is in private practice in Greenwich, Connecticut. She has consulted with local schools and was an active charter member of the special education section of the Greenwich Parent-Teacher Association. In addition, she developed and facilitated the Learning Differences Network for the Junior League of Greenwich in conjunction with Greenwich Hospital. She also serves as facilitator for "The Parent Exchange" with Greenwich Hospital. Aronsson is also a guest lecturer and consultant at area schools and Parents Together, an organization sponsored by local public and independent schools.